The hills are theirs

Larry Batson

The hills are theirs

Tales from the Ozarks

 Published by the Minneapolis Tribune
Minneapolis Star and Tribune Company
425 Portland Av. / Minneapolis / Minn. / 55488

Larry Batson's columns, first published in the Minneapolis
Tribune, have been slightly revised and edited for this book.

First Printing

Library of Congress Cataloging in Publication Data
Batson, Larry, 1930-
The hills are theirs.

1. Batson, Larry, 1930-   2. Sportswriters—
United States—Biography.   I. Title.
GV719.B37A33   070.4'092'4   [B]   78-15997

ISBN 0-932272-01-0

Design / Michael Carroll
Illustrations / L. K. Hanson
Compositor / TriStar Graphics

To Laurel

Author's note/

These are tales I heard from my family and people I knew. Or they are personal experiences as I remember them. If I come off well, it is probably because I shaded the truth a little in my favor. Those who passed stories along to me probably exercised the same option. One other thing: Economic tides, which always seemed to be ebbing, deposited me and my parents in five different communities during the period covered by this book. I have not attempted to sort that out. Friends may think they have found themselves between these covers. Could be, but more than likely it was another person in another place.

Contents

1/Anchored to bedrock

My family has resisted the Industrial Revolution with Churchillian doggedness, recognizing early on that progress is a snare and a delusion that leads inevitably to regular employment.

Swept from their comfortable stews beside the Thames by some forgotten cataclysm, my ancestors took root in what was to become West Virginia. Since then such developments as the Whisky Rebellion, the popularization of the steam engine and modern mining and milling methods have pushed them back into the mountains of Tennessee and Kentucky, the Ozark region of Arkansas and Missouri and the badlands of Oklahoma.

They are in all of those places today, dug in on rocky slopes and in the deep woods just beyond the lapping flood of civilization. Some have converted to the work ethic, but in many the flame of resistance still burns fiercely.

Not that they do not labor. Many of them work very hard. But they do not willingly put their hand to another man's plow nor march to an employer's cadence count.

My grandfather once whipped a village marshal at the request of a merchant. The storekeeper gave grandfather a pair of overalls. That, in all his 90 years, was as close as grandfather came to hiring out for wages.

Two cousins of mine decided to "work for the public," which in hill terms means any job that involves taking orders from another person or coming in contact with

strangers on any terms but your own. My cousins were hired at a small factory to melt down scrap metal. The furnace at which they worked had to reach a certain temperature before it could be used. Something to do with removal of impurities.

For 10 days my cousins leaned on their shovels. The furnace never reached operating temperature. Inspectors pronounced it in perfect condition. Still, it never got hot enough. My cousins grew careless. Somebody caught them rigging a hose. For 10 days they had been running cold water into the back of the furnace.

Let it not be said that my people are immune to the nobler impulses. They have done their bit. My great-grandfather, so they say, jumped bounty on both sides of the Civil War.

My people, the hill people, live by a code that is all the stronger for being unwritten, unspoken and sometimes supremely illogical. We walk stiff-backed and wary; we speak softly and indirectly—for bluntness is discourteous—and we will, on occasion, march open-eyed off a cliff.

When a doctor from Illinois, who had bought the old Buchanan place, saw Bump Crowder's cows straying, he penned them. That evening he flagged down Bump's car and told him succinctly that his cows were loose, that his fence was down, that he had corralled the cows, and that

Bump should fix his fence.

Bump took this as intolerable officiousness. First, he knew the danged things were out. That's why he was driving around at supper time, as even a big-mouth from Illinois should have realized. And of course the fence was down. That's how they got out. But Bump would patch his own fence in his own good time, not by the say-so of some furriner. Finally, you don't pen another man's livestock if there is any way out of it. That has led to all sorts of trouble, some of it fatal.

Bump said nothing. He opened the doctor's gate, drove his cows back on the road and let them scatter. Then Bump went home. His cows ran loose all night. Bump's grandsons had the devil of a time rounding them up.

Tens of thousands of people have moved into the Ozarks since I left them. Older people who bought retirement homes, younger ones attracted by cheap land, workers for the scores of small factories that have sprung up.

I tell myself that life there will have changed, that the children of the hill people I knew will have turned into the flabby sort of conformist I have become, working for wages and taking other men's orders. But I visit and all seems much as it was when I left. The towns are larger. The townfolk are sleeker. The hill people drive new pickup trucks and work in the new plants.

But all that is irrelevant. The hill people have no objection to affluence. But it has come to them, and they accept it on their own terms. They walk and talk and live as they always have. They remain with their own and in their hills, anchored to bedrock.

The year of the heavy rains when Dripping Springs Lake filled up and held water all summer our family had its finest Fourth of July in modern times. There had been nothing to equal it since the summer day both wives of one of my ancestors showed up at the same camp meeting.

A ghastly breakdown of communications, that. My ancestor, a stock buyer who spent most of his time traveling, thought one wife would be at the camp meeting and the other at another gathering 20 miles away. He had a fast horse.

When he rode into the campgrounds, both wives' wagons were parked in the same oak grove. Two women, two broods of children and two sets of inlaws were waiting.

"Warn't a word spoke," said my grandfather, whom we called Poppy. "Somebody eared back the hammers of a shotgun. Slater reached real slow into his coat pocket and pulled out his poke (purse). Stock buyers carried a lot of money, mostly gold coin.

"He dropped the poke on the ground, reined his horse around and lit out. In three jumps that horse was belly to the ground and tail straight out behind. I don't believe I ever saw a finer piece of horseflesh."

Poppy was 13 years old when that man rode south. It was his last glimpse of his father.

Poppy was talking softly to the menfolk and older boys. We were stretched out on the grassy bank of the big pond, where we would sleep. Frogs chanted on the far side of the pond. The women and smaller children were in the house. Lights were still on downstairs and we could hear laughter now and again.

"Not but one wife apiece in this gang," said my Uncle Lurvy when Poppy had finished his story. "More than enough, I'd say."

"None for me," stuck in Charley Ray, Lurvy's son, and Lurvy countered dryly, "Zerelda might have a notion about changing that."

"Oh shoot," said Charley Ray. "I'd just take my foot in hand and bid her a fond farewell."

I stored that remark for later use. Charley Ray was a man of the world and I admired his style.

He was on leave from the Navy and had brought his girlfriend to the gathering. Zerelda arrived wearing shorts and everybody took notice, especially my grandmother, who gasped when those endless bare legs slid out of the car. Grandmother's skirts touched her shoes. After a while, Zerelda had gone upstairs and put on a skirt.

Charley Ray had a Ford automobile with mudflaps on each fender, a squirrel tail on the antenna and a black, imitation onyx, eight-ball gearshift knob. He carried a pack of Luckies rolled in one T-shirt sleeve and called us kids "swabbies."

He told tales of Navy life and, looking at the night sky, of navigating by stars. Charley Ray was a baker and spent his whole hitch on a ship tied up in the Bremerton Navy Yard, but he sort of skipped over that part.

Morning chores were more of a festival than work with so many hands competing for the tasks, and the food started coming at breakfast and never quit. There was all the usual stuff and the special things, too. There was a cream can full of ice tea and another of lemonade. The old galvanized iron watering tank was full of watermelons and chunk ice. Charley Ray and Zerelda drove to town, returned with five gallons of ice cream and disappeared again.

We rode the horses—none the equal of that stock buyer's mount—shot at targets, talked and snoozed in the shade. About midday we loaded a truck with food and moved down to Dripping Springs.

All that part of the Ozarks is underlaid with limestone. Sinkholes, caverns and underground streams abound. Maybe 40 years earlier the bottom of the lake had sunk into one of those layers of limestone and Dripping Springs hadn't held water again until this summer. Now it was 15 feet deep out in the middle, clear as crystal and perfect.

There were the usual water fights, near-drownings, flirtations, snake scares and horror stories of children who had overeaten, cramped into knots and sunk without trace.

At dusk Cousin Dee Boy set up fireworks he'd bought from a bootleg stand. It was a fine show.

At last we were quiet, watching the moon rise over the water and listening to the whippoorwills.

Charley Ray's Ford made the turn from the road in a spray of gravel and stopped in our midst. He was grinning like a possum. Zerelda looked demurely at her feet.

"We done it," Charley Ray announced. "We're married."

"Querencia" is the Spanish word for that particular patch of country to which a longhorn cow clung, to which she would return if she escaped from a drive hundreds of miles up the trail. Or it can be a man's homeplace, the spot to which he will return if he can, the only place in which he feels truly comfortable.

My father's querencia was a little dab of the Ozarks. Roughly bounded on the east and south by the James River bottoms and breaks, on the north by the old sorghum mill near Bois d'Arc to which he drove wagons of cane to be made into molasses, it extended west to the cabin of my great-great-grandfather.

"The Original Slater," we call that ancestor because he led the clan into Missouri. The stone chimney of his cabin, built before the Civil War, still stands near Halltown beside Hwy. 66, its fireplace usually choked with weeds. Slater Batson was murdered in front of that fireplace, shot in the back by Jayhawkers who rode up at night, posing as new neighbors, and asked to borrow a horse. Slater returned his rifle to the pegs above his cabin door and stepped into the light to take a bridle down from the mantel.

Every new generation is shown the chimney and told the tale. As recently as 1940, when asked whether anybody ever caught those Jayhawkers, my grandfather replied, "Not yet."

My grandfather considered himself to be a just man, but when he was angered, retribution was swift and terrible.

My grandmother shopped around for salvation, drifting from one country preacher to another. Grandfather made no fuss. "You can pray with 'em and feed 'em," he would say, "but keep 'em away from me."

That she did until she took up with a splinter group that had no meeting place. Grandfather had recently bought at auction a vacated country school and grandmother wheedled him out of it for Sunday meetings. Then she brought the preacher home for dinner. That chap, abrim with gratitude, overflowed all over grandfather's quiet afternoon.

The next day grandfather drove to Springfield and sold the schoolhouse to a home-moving firm. He stipulated that it had to be jacked up and hauled away before the next Sabbath. It was.

That story is told, of course, at every family gathering. A granddaughter of one of that preacher's followers once told me the version of the incident that survives in her family. Quite some difference. "Never trust a Batson," is the tag line and moral.

My father was 13 when he made his first trip alone to the sorghum mill. It took half a day to drive the wagon there and he camped at the site for two nights.

The cane was crushed in a big press, which was turned by horse power—old, steady beasts that walked a weary circle day and night until all the cane was processed. The sweet juice ran out into a trough, then into barrels. It would be strained and cooked into light syrup and dark gummy blackstrap.

The mill owner was a master hand at cooking the syrup. He took his pay in cash or the product. But syrup making was really a social event. People tended the fires all night, fiddlers played, kids slept on quilts in wagons or on pallets in the house or barnloft. There were dances and pancake feeds and fights and shooting matches and horse races.

My father wasn't much of a shot, but he was good at everything else. For his first 23 years he roved his querencia, the last seven years always on Ribbon, an outlawed horse that he had gentled. Nobody else ever rode Ribbon. When my father left home, he gave him to his favorite brother, my Uncle Lurvy.

My father was a master hand with horses. He gentled an 8-year-old outlaw mule for Jimmy Walker, a beast that had crippled men. When my father finished, the mule followed him like a pet dog. He learned, and told me often, that nothing on earth is as stubborn as a "sully mule." When a mule sulls, it can be moved only by building a fire under it.

Then it might move only far enough to escape the flame.

Boxing matches were a feature of every church or family picnic, every fair and carnival in those days. For years my father was unbeaten. Often he would ride Ribbon from one picnic to another and fight three or four times on a Sunday. Once with Lurvy and other friends watching the timekeeper to ensure a fair count, my father fought a carnival boxer to a standstill and won $10.

That was at a little town named Battlefield, on the site of the Battle of Wilson Creek. From the Battlefield postoffice my father mailed a letter answering a magazine advertisement for a course in auto mechanics, then a glamorous and exciting career. He proved to be a master mechanic, too. In a short time he acquired a motorcycle, joined a troupe of barnstorming racers and hill-climbers. He rode in races and boxed all comers for several years all over the South and in the cowtowns and mining camps of the West. In Colorado he met my mother.

He worked for a long time in Colorado, but not willingly. Each time he had saved enough, he would return to the Ozarks and open a little garage. Several times he was driven back west, broke. Eventually though, he made enough to elevate his little farm and a repair shop to subsistence level. He spent his last two decades near his querencia, at peace.

––––––––––––

Uncle Lurvy believed that man was put on earth to hunt, to fish and to sire enough children to handle the chores. Several times a year when work piled up to a point where it could no longer be comfortably ignored, Lurvy would head for the woods, usually with a crony.

Outfitting one of Lurvy's camping trips was simple. Into the back of his pickup he threw tarpaulins, quilts, a big iron skillet, a big iron kettle, a graniteware coffeepot, some piepans to eat off, a sack of onions and potatoes, a bag of coffee, a small crock of lard and a sack of cornmeal and flour mixed together.

The last, but most definitely indispensable, item to be tossed into the back of the truck was the nearest able-bodied kid dumb enough to hang around and watch.

Lurvy liked to get back where the woods hadn't been shot over or the streams fished out. He would park his truck as close as possible, then he and his buddy would hike in, toting shotguns and fishing rods. The kid followed with a load of camp gear. He might make two or three trips.

For the next two or three days the kid never got 10 yards from the campsite. He cut wood, cleaned fish and game, cooked and washed up.

What Lurvy and his pal shot and caught was fried or put into the pot where it simmered with potatoes and onions. That flour and cornmeal mixture was made into batter and fried. Lumps of it were dropped into grease that had been used to fry rabbit, squirrel or catfish and toasted into golden brown hushpuppies that would gag a goat. Lurvy loved 'em.

In the evening, pleasantly tired and with his belly full, Lurvy would lie back against a rolled tarpaulin while the kid fetched a burning twig to light his pipe.

"This is the way man was meant to live," Lurvy would chuckle.

The hills are getting too crowded to suit Uncle Olen. Twenty-five years ago when he took over the home place, it was 15 miles to the city, five to a crossroads store. Olen put up with those intimations of a distant civilization because of the convenience.

As for instance, the time he lost a leg in a silage cutter. He wrapped the stump in his shirt, fashioned a tourniquet from his belt and hopped half a mile to the house. "Lost a leg," he told his wife. "I reckon I better doctor for it."

One of the children rode horseback to the store, got a neighbor with a pickup to haul Olen to the city and less than six hours after the accident, he was in a hospital. "Handy," Olen admitted.

He even bought a car after that incident. And so did most of his sons. They had had tractors for years and could all drive. Olen just didn't care to and naturally his wishes decided the matter for the whole family. The boys even got licenses. I doubt that Olen ever bothered. I can't conceive of any lawman down home making a point of it with Olen.

A few years after he lost his leg, Olen walked into a nest of copperheads in the woods. He was bitten many times before he could get his knife out, kill the snakes and slash all the bites to let them bleed. It took him three hours to get to the house that time, covered with blood and "swole up like a poisoned pup."

Without a car and a paved road a few miles away, Olen would have died. Again he admitted that these refinements were handy. But that was years ago and now the disadvantages of what is becoming surburban life outweigh the conveniences.

There are water mains within 15 miles of his place. Rich city people are building estates within five miles. Olen could sell all or part of his land and be as rich as the people who are crowding him, if he isn't already.

Most hill people are desperately poor, but some of them amass astonishing holdings by the simple expedient of never spending anything. They tuck it away in country banks or buy more land. Olen, I suspect, is one of those.

You can't tell these people by their way of life. They never discuss their holdings. A direct question is unthinkable. Hill people live alike, dress alike, work alike.

A man named Charlie, a neighbor of ours, who is known to own several thousand acres and, with his children, a great amount of business and residential property in half a dozen towns, once bought a feeder steer from my brother, who was liquidating my father's estate. It was a wild, uncatchable animal, blind in one eye, the last animal left on the farm.

Charlie paid $75 for the steer. He brought two of his sons-in-law, horses, ropes and a truck to capture the steer. It took the three of them most of a day. Three men who run many farms, a truck line, a sawmill, several businesses. They sold the steer that evening for $100. "Like finding money," Charlie said. It is permissible in the hills to brag a little on a successful deal.

My grandfather, whose land Olen now owns, once took me along as he sold a bunch of hogs, several truckloads. He caught the top of the market in Springfield, receiving something like $8,000. He took the money in cash, bought a can of salmon and a bushel of eating apples. On the way home, he stopped for water at an acquaintance's place and traded half the apples for two angora goats. He didn't mention the hogs when we got home, but described every step of his negotiations for those goats. One of his better swaps.

Except for a couple of trips across the country as a young buck and service in the Pacific during World War II, Olen has never left the hills. He seldom leaves his own land. But he walks and rides his own hills and woods and creeks endlessly. He gets around so well that you can't tell one leg is artificial.

Olen can't see the houses of the city people who are crowding him. Not yet. "But I can feel them," he said. When he goes to the store, there's likely to be a station wagon parked out front. The first time Olen saw a man wearing a leisure suit, he drove home and sat by the fireplace for a long time. He described the man's garb and shook his head in disgust.

A few days later he drove off into the hills. He bought 300 acres deep in the woods. There are cliffs and caves, some meadow land. Ridges and two rivers seal it off. There is one road in and Olen owns it.

He has repaired the house and barn and is piping water from an unfailing spring. He will leave a son to run the home place, which has been in the family for 150 years, and to cope with the oncoming city people.

"I'll not be back," he said. "They ain't got airy thing I want."

2/Poppy: the patriarch

When he tore down my grandfather's house, Uncle Lurvy
looped a chain around a couple of logs in the original cabin
part and gave one tug with his tractor. The whole structure
groaned wearily and collapsed slowly into a pitiful heap of
scraps, like an old, old man lowering himself into bed.

Much of the debris sank into the cellar, a long, narrow
trench grubbed out of the clay and gravel hillside more than
a hundred years before. Exposed to sunlight, the cellar was
small and unimpressive, but to generations of children who
had descended gingerly the rickety steps from the summer
kitchen, it had been a terrifying place.

For 50 years or more my grandmother had fed an endless
stream of canned food into that cellar. Fruits, vegetables,
sausage and other meats—fried, packed into half-gallon
Mason or Ball jars and covered with its own grease—
anything and everything that would serve as a hedge
against the near-starvation she and my grandfather had
known a few times.

Long after the need had passed, when the old people were
alone and their children were prospering, or at least surviv-
ing, on their own places, grandmother kept on canning,
frying, drying, preserving. She would carry down quarts of
peaches or jellies and make room for them on the rotting oak
shelves by clearing out jars of fruit or preserves that had
spoiled 10 years earlier.

When there was a child in the house, as usually there was,
visiting for a week or a month or half a year, helping with

chores, keeping the old folks company, that child would fetch whatever grandmother called for.

You would descend slowly into that black pit, holding a kerosene lamp out front and a stick in your other hand, in case another copperhead, fat, sluggish, evil-tempered and swollen with poison, had found its way inside. There would be cobwebs everywhere. You were sure to walk into one blindly then suck in your breath in horror. You would find the right jar, tuck your stick under your lamp arm and get out as quickly as possible, heart beating wildly.

Upstairs again there would be light and warmth and familiar things to erase the terror. Grandfather, whom we called "Poppy," in his ancient hickory rocker sitting by the heating stove. A box of ashes in front, winter or summer, for spitting. A pile of traps in the corner or a piece of harness to mend and a stack of magazines.

There was a long table brought by grandmother's folks from Kentucky. A bench held together by wooden pegs that my great-grandfather Slater made before he took off on the high lonesome, leaving Poppy, a teen-ager, in possession of farm, family and responsibilities. The bench seated two children, three at a pinch.

On whittled pegs above the door of the main room rested

Poppy's old black shotgun. When callers came, they stopped in the yard and hollered. Grandfather would open the door, one hand overhead on his shotgun. Hill people's manners. Even today it's best to stop and call out at a stranger's house.

Originally the house was a cabin of two rooms, three if you counted the lean-to that became the summer kitchen. As the family grew, rooms were tacked on any old how. There were lots of rooms eventually, some just large enough for a cot, others fairly commodious.

Time available and the material at hand dictated the size and location. I don't think any two floors were on the same level. To get to one room, you had to go through Poppy's bedroom, through Grandmother's room and through one used for storage. My father and Lurvy built themselves a bedroom that couldn't be reached from inside the house. You went out and around. One Christmas visit when both were in their forties, they cut a door through the summer kitchen wall into their old room. They slept in the room that night and were quite pleased with themselves. "I got some other chores I been savin' for 35 years," Poppy said.

The house was on a steep hill, above it the barn and cow lot, beside it pigsty and chicken house and an outside toilet. Down below all of them, getting the drainage, was the hand-dug well from which the family's water was taken with a big cedar bucket and a rope on a windlass. Four of Poppy's sons lived to manhood. Several other children died in infancy. "Fever took them," grandmother would say.

People in need went to their kinfolk in those days more than now. One old man came to Poppy and Grandma with a letter from a preacher in Oklahoma indicating that he was related to one of them. He was senile and had a crippled leg. He was quiet, amiable, like a small, friendly child. We never did figure out the exact relationship so we settled for calling him Uncle Jim and he lived with my grandparents until he died.

After he pulled down Poppy's house, Uncle Lurvy drove to his own place, a house with an air-conditioner in the win-

dow, a television antenna on the roof, running water inside.
Lurvy went to the old privy he'd kept when the pipes were
run inside. He sat there for quite a while and cried a little.
Then he took his wife to the movies.

───────────────────

Most of the time my grandfather enjoyed exceedingly his
life as patriarch of an undistinguished Ozark clan. He was
especially pleased when his kinfolk locked in dispute and he
could busy himself as peacemaker.

Poppy was unorthodox but usually effective. He once settled
a fuss between two cousins over division of a corn crop by
chasing one of them up into the barn loft and keeping him
there all night.

Every so often grandfather would fire a shotgun blast
through the loft floor. This kept the lines of communication
open, as labor relations experts like to say. At dawn, just as
he was about to become an unmissable target, the cousin
agreed that there was much in what Poppy had to say.

Another time my great-uncle Tom sat at Sunday dinner in
grandfather's house and refused to consider a compromise
put forth by Poppy.

"Hain't there airy thing I can say to change your mind?"
grandfather asked. Tom shook his head stubbornly.

My grandfather leaped across the table, knocked Tom to the
floor, knelt on him and began choking him blue. Tom
blinked his bulging eyes in acquiescence.

However, life does not provide many such splendid oppor-
tunities for unfettered diplomacy. And when existence in
the bosom of his family grew "teejus," Poppy was apt to
disappear from sight for weeks on end.

When Poppy, rocking in front of the stove and spitting pensively into the box of wood ashes, sighed and sang softly, "I'm a-goin' down to some big town—and swing the gals around," you knew that his heart was full. Serenity was galling him. Next line in the old ditty is "Then I'll buy myself a half a pint—and sleep in the wagon yard."

Poppy used to say, "I only know two songs. One of 'em's 'Dixie' and the other ain't." But he actually knew a lot of them. "Long About the Time That They're Sweet Sixteen" and "Cotton-Eyed Joe" were favorites. A roguish old devil, was Poppy.

At such times, the family sometimes attached a grandson or great-grandson to Poppy as sort of a sea anchor to keep him from drifting too far. They reckoned he wouldn't abandon a kid or lead him astray. The boy might lose a little sleep, but Poppy would bring him home before too long.

This worked pretty well, although Poppy once deposited my Uncle Lurvy and a whole stalk of bananas on a neighbor's wagon. Lurvy loved bananas, and by the time the neighbor dropped him at home, he'd eaten much of the stalk and was in a stupor. He had no idea where Poppy was.

Once my grandmother thwarted Poppy's gypsy impulses for a month or more and he was growing sulkier by the hour. Grandma chose that time to reopen an ancient grievance. In 50-odd years, Poppy had never given her a birthday present. His stand was that nobody deserved a decoration for lasting another year, especially considering the alternative.

This time grandma got some action. Poppy went to town and bought a big pink granite tombstone with her name and birthdate carved on it. Besides that, Poppy said, he'd already paid "for the rest of the work—one more date."

By nightfall grandma had gathered a dozen or more scandalized kinfolk around her, all come to see for themselves. It wasn't the sort of thing you accepted on hearsay.

The women were in the kitchen, comforting grandma. The

men sat in a stunned circle around Poppy, who was rocking and spitting.

Poppy smiled softly and started humming "Sleep in the Wagon Yard."

"Let him go!" shrieked grandma. "Let the old fool go!"

Each holiday season Poppy would gather the clan. Usually his summons was both piteous and imperious, scrawled shakily with indelible pencil on a postcard.

"One last look at my loved ones before My Maker gathers me to His bosom" was my all-time favorite. Poppy was about 60 when he wrote that, with 32 strong white teeth, his hair black and crisply curling. He stood 6-foot-3, straight as the hickory shoot he used to clean his old black shotgun and just as lean and limber.

Even my father had to laugh. It would be 10 years before Poppy's hair turned gray and 30 before his maker summoned him. And I guarantee you nobody gathered Poppy to his bosom. Maybe a handshake and a howdy.

What Poppy intended, we knew, was to reaffirm his role as patriarch. There would be a strict accounting. Adults who had been throwing away money on fripperies like low-cut shoes or had been out honky-tonking would answer. So would women who were using lip rouge or bobbing their hair—Poppy's terms for any cosmetic or styling effort. Youngsters, the twigs of the family tree, would be rebent in the proper direction and frozen into it.

There was no boogeyman in our family. A sassy kid could be paralyzed with "What if Poppy found out?" The awful thing was that he always did. You would be called to stand before his ancient rocker. Poppy's gray eyes would fasten on yours. An icicle of fear would transfix your liver. "I hear you got yourself a new bicycle tire (dreadful pause) without no money." Oh, Lord, gather ME to your bosom! Right now!

There would be feasting and bickering and gossiping, hunting and swapping and amiable division of chores, mostly discussions by adults of whose kids were going to do them. And there would be one great feast at which Poppy would offer his annual prayer for the well being of the clan. He would combine it with his last will and testament.

Every flat surface would be covered with trays, platters, bowls, pans, pots, crocks, jars and stacks of food. The aroma would be maddening as Poppy prayed and prayed and prayed. No peccadillo of the previous year was skipped, no secret was safe, no violation of the family code escaped notice. Serious transgressions of 20 years earlier were replayed.

"Give Charley Clyde strength, O Lord, to resist the wiles of them painted sluts in beer joints," Poppy would quaver. "Let him remember that he has a sweet, wonderful, hard-workin' woman and nine kiddies. And when You take me, I want Charley Clyde to have the roan cow, the three-quartered one."

Last year Charley Clyde had got the tractor. This codicil cancelled that bequest. He would be properly abashed.

Fence line disputes, religious arguments, minor squabbles were settled by fiat. Candidates for township, county and school district offices were endorsed. Nagging, lip rouge, one grandson's "bob-legged britches" (worn only that summer in a town 500 miles away) were sternly admonished.

No one fidgeted. That just brought the offender into the prayer and lengthened it. Poppy had eyebrows like briar patches and from beneath them his gray eyes would drill through the brisket of a restless clansman. Heads would turn and for the next five minutes as Poppy dealt with the offender, the clan would unite in one emotion: undiluted hatred.

Grandmother stood patiently behind Poppy until he finished. Then she would step into the kitchen and drop two or three pans to the floor, noisily.

Poppy enjoyed his imaginary ill health enormously. He would begin breakfast, for example, with a cup of Postum and some noxious gruel that he had heard advertised on radio. Then he would piece out the meal with several huge biscuits covered with cream gravy, six or eight eggs, sausage, fried pork, fruit, jam, pie and lots of coffee. That held him until noon dinner, his big meal.

Sometime during the visit there would be a wagon ride with Poppy to the cornfield. Several grandchildren, the farm dogs and cats would go along. Children would load corn and pumpkins. The animals would kill the mice that ran from under the corn.

Poppy always had a field of properly shocked corn, though most of the crop was picked by machine. The corn was cut with long knives or short, curved ones. Shocks were begun by twisting together two or three uncut stalks, then more corn was stacked around them tepee fashion. The whole thing was held together by other stalks twisted into a rope. Pumpkins were piled around the shocks.

Every visitor received one or two pumpkins, usually huge

things that would make a dozen or more pies. If a woman protested, she got another pumpkin. Poppy hated pumpkins.

"Wulp," Poppy would say to his team of horses and they would start ahead. "Wulp," and they would turn left or right as desired. "Wulp," and they stopped. Poppy never twitched the reins. Aren't you supposed to say Gee and Haw and Whoa? a grandchild asked. "Wulp," Poppy explained.

There would be evenings of talk around the big wood-burning heating stove. Arguments broke out occasionally. When Poppy's voice deepened, a son or mature grandson would edge between him and the door. Poppy's shotgun rested above it.

When enraged, and it didn't take long, Poppy would leap for the gun. One man would snatch it away and two or three others would pin Poppy to the floor until he subsided.

In early years, those fireside chats were "gen-you-wine chair-busters," Uncle Lurvy remembers, and Poppy might have to be choked till he turned blue. After Poppy passed 75, the boys would shuffle feet and wave arms to give him time to scramble to his feet, then puff and grunt and make a great to-do about holding him down. It saved his pride.

One small grandson usually shared Poppy's bed when the house was crowded. There would be six to eight quilts atop the feather mattress, all impregnated with the smell of Poppy's liniment and pipe tobacco. A kid under that stack of quilts was immobilized like a butterfly under glass.

Poppy would smoke his pipe and listen to his radio—music and evangelists from outlaw stations in Mexico and Del Rio, Texas. He'd come wide awake when a new health treatment was mentioned, then settle back.

Finally he would grunt and switch off the radio. Silence would descend over the old house.

When Poppy, our Tamerlane, called, we went. Sometimes the summons caught us in Colorado, where Pop would be working as a mechanic to get together a stake. Our last trek back to the Ozarks from the Rockies coincided with one of Poppy's holiday calls. Pop had accumulated an enormous stake, more than $1,500. In the end, it proved enough to keep him in the Ozarks, working hard until the day he died, but at home.

This was during World War II and the gold mines in the mountains had been shut down. Pop bought an old truck, a 1933 Chevrolet, from one mining outfit and fixed it for our trip. He, my mother and my sister rode in the cab. My dog Ricky and I rode in back with all our belongings, in a little space at the tailgate padded with quilts. The truck's top speed loaded was 25 miles an hour, but Pop held it under that. We had 1,200 miles to travel.

There are better ways to travel than riding backward, peering through the cracks of a tailgate. You can't read the billboards or the Burma Shave signs. You can't see much of anything. If there is a tailwind and blowing snow, as there was most of the way, you lapse into a gelid stupor. I sang, I cried, I thought of ingenious ways to murder those responsible for my plight. I thought of slipping off when the truck labored up a hill, making my fortune, returning home and then killing everyone.

We stopped for breakfast, a bowl of oatmeal, and Pop announced that he would drive as far as he could before halting again. My mother had made meatloaf sandwiches. She gave me two and told me to eat them at noon. I finished the second one at 8:30 a.m. Pop stopped for gas after dark that day. Ricky was helped out and streaked for a tree. We got gas, visited restrooms, talked a bit and prepared to leave. Ricky smiled weakly, apologetically from that tree. He still wasn't finished.

On the second day as we neared a city, Topeka, I think, I tried another sandwich. Its age, the cold, the motion and my mood made me sick. I unfastened the tarpaulin covering the cargo, leaned over the tailgate and vomited. The flapping canvas alerted Pop. He stopped, put my sister in back and me up front to recover. We drove slowly through the city and stopped for gas. A car had been following us. It stopped, too, and the woman in it asked my sister how long she had been riding there. "Two days and a night," my sister said, sounding like the Little Match Girl. The woman gave her some cookies, a candy bar and a quarter. My sister climbed back in the cab. Twenty miles, that hateful girl had ridden in back!

Most of the family had reached Poppy's farm ahead of us. As always, there were a number of elderly ladies who arrived looking curiously bulky, bloated. They wore many dresses, one atop another. When one became wrinkled or spotted, after a nap, perhaps, they would remove it and be presentable again. One woman was rather vague. She introduced herself to each adult and quizzed each child after every nap.

Uncle Lurvy's wife had died a year before in a fire. He brought his many children, a widow he was courting and later married, and her many children.

Uncle Olen was home on furlough in a buck private's uniform. The war was discussed and Olen, with three months of service, was the final authority. He took his .22 rifle from its pegs and handed it to me. "What's that?" "A rifle," I replied. "No sir, that's a weapon. It is your friend. It is your life." He put me through the manual of arms.

Every so often Grandmother would look at Olen, sob and dry her eyes with her apron.

Poppy and his sons walked the fields in silence mostly, but occasionally reminding each other of the long ago. There was a feast, or rather a series of them. "Lydia put the little pot in the big one," Poppy would say after each meal.

For Christmas I got a Dick Tracy Big-Little Book. In one corner were drawings of Tracy disarming a thug. Flip the pages and it was like a movie. Poppy had bought a sack of oranges.

Lurvy, dead broke with seven, soon to be 12, kids to feed. Pop, 40 years old and hoping to hang on to a farm this time after three failures. Olen, scared but dreaming of glory. They had the best seats around the fire.

"Wonder what kind of day ol' John D. Rockefeller had," Lurvy drawled. "I figure when a man gets a pile of money, it changes him. Got to worry about who's going to take it away."

"Yeah," said Pop, "I'd rather be poor. Wouldn't you?"

"Nope," said Lurvy.

"Me neither," said Pop.

3/Country living

This fellow asked whereabouts a man could have a quiet drink and sort things out. Had a troubled mind, he said, and needed to think. I was pleased to oblige.

Take the old Brookline Road out of Springfield, Missouri, I told him, drive toward Battlefield and then swing north toward Bois d'Arc as far as the old sorghum mill. The mill hasn't been used since the 1920s, but anyone can tell you how to get there.

Then you turn down the hill to Pickerel Creek, to where it gushes out from a limestone cliff into a grove of sycamore trees. Up the hill a ways is the old church and graveyard. On the uphill bank watercress flourishes in summertime. There are patches of wild mint on the downhill bank. They stay green all winter.

On the way you'll pass Herman Rickett's farm. Sort of a shirt-tail cousin of my father, Herman is. A good farmer, but he owes his prosperity to a buckskin stallion, a crazy outlaw beast that died years back but sired a notable line of bucking horses first. Rodeo buyers still come to pick the roughest of that old stud's descendants. That's why you'll find high, strong fences around the place. Horse high, bull stout and hog tight, the Ozark description is. Herman needs 'em.

Glen Batson runs the store near the Frisco Railroad siding. You'll pass it. Glen's son, of the same first name, is a wolf hunter. They call coyotes and coydogs, the crossbred, feral predators, wolves down there. Young Glen, the wolves and the poultry farmers maintain a natural equilibrium. Glen

kills enough wolves to keep the farmers in business. The wolves never get so thick that the government might send in trappers to eradicate them. Nobody gets rich, but all involved survive.

Pickerel Creek has cut a deep pool in its first rush to freedom. In summer, the pool swarms with fish, frogs and crayfish—crawdads, we call them. In winter, there is just the sound of the water to keep you company, and the scrape of the sycamore boughs.

The creek flattens out a little bit and runs westward through a meadow. At the far end of it, there are the remains of an old gristmill, built before the Civil War and falling apart now. You can see the corner of the Harrelson place just beyond the mill.

In years past, the Harrelsons raised geese. They would build string fences out of little pegs and white twine to guide those geese to their wheat or barley fields in the springtime. Maybe six inches high, just one string on top of the stakes, but the geese would stay inside. They would spread out over the grainfield, eating the weeds. At dusk, they'd come back home for a little corn. At a certain age, the geese were plucked for down. Never seemed to bother them. They'd waddle around with bare briskets until a new crop of down grew in. The Harrelsons sold it to pillow makers.

All over the meadow you'll see remains of a pestilential weed with sticky leaves and lots of little white flowers. Lu Miller weed, people call it. Lu Miller was a widow woman, a decent, kind person and a good neighbor, but the weed first appeared on her farm 50 years ago and that's how she is remembered.

Downstream and uphill, you can see the rooftop and corner of a rock house. Another widow and her pretty daughter once lived there. Took up with a couple of motorcycle riders one summer. Those old boys liked to play electric guitars. They'd ride out from Springfield at night and set up amplifiers on the hilltop. Spook horses and cattle and set foxhounds to baying for miles around. When the widow's riding horse and colt broke loose one midnight, the boyfriends tried to round them up on their motorcycles in the dark. One hit a fence; the other didn't see a clothesline in time. Served them right, everybody said.

On westward, the creek empties into the Sac River. My patchy reading of American history generally refers to the Sac Indians as a peaceable, no-account tribe. That's what the Sioux thought, too, when they moved into Sac territory. The Sac chased 'em 700 miles.

The Frisco line doesn't invade the meadow. It runs several miles north, but far off on a crisp day you sometimes hear the Cannonball on its way to Kansas City. A fellow we'll call Hake tried to derail the Cannonball once. He and some buddies piled old ties on the tracks and hid in the brush on a hillside to see the fun. The Cannonball chuffed around a curve and gently nudged the ties out of its path. It stopped and the engineer climbed down and hollered, "Hake, you fan your sorry tail down here and clear this trash off the right of way. Any more tricks like this and I'm gonna talk to your daddy."

Now about that drink. The water in that deep pool is the same temperature the year around, cold enough to hurt your teeth and cramp your stomach if you gulp it. On a cold day, you'll want to sit at the foot of a sycamore, warm, dry and sheltered by the cliff and trees, and build a fire in one of the rings of smoke-blackened stones. Boil some coffee and look down the creek and sort things out.

I hope that fellow finds the place. Some days I miss it so much I could bawl.

Snow didn't fall very often in our part of the Ozarks, maybe two or three times a winter. But when it did, the school buses would be half-empty. The kids were needed at home to hunt rabbits.

Fried or stewed, rabbits made a nice addition to a winter diet of side meat. And extra ones could be sold for 50 cents apiece at Richards Brothers store, where most of the big hunts were planned.

Richards was a fabulously successful general store. All of the necessities and most of the luxuries of life were stacked, stored, piled or crammed together on its shelves, in bins or barrels, in bales or the cartons they were delivered in maybe 10 years earlier. Nothing was thrown away or taken out of stock.

You could buy liners for heating stoves—do you know what those are?—10 tons of hog feed, velvet for a party dress (the feed sacks made school dresses), coal oil for your lantern, crepe paper to decorate the schoolhouse for a pie supper, a ring for your bull's nose—anything the human heart might covet.

Chewing tobacco was kept in a closed glass case. Everything else was out in the open for handling and comparison. There were benches where you could sit and ponder, a box of sawdust to spit in, "accommodations" for the ladies in a neat little room to the back. Men could walk down the street and use the restroom at the filling station.

When the prospect of snow was in the air, hunters would gather to buy shells for their shotguns and talk over the likely places. Best spots were where somebody had cleared a considerable patch of timber long enough ago for the brush piles to settle down into good rabbit cover. Sprouts, grasses and brush would have grown up around them, providing food.

Sometimes a scouting party would go out. That could be dangerous in the Dripping Springs, White Church, Peace Valley area, where we lived. Bump Crowder owned those roads.

Bump was about 80 and he couldn't see more than eight feet. Nobody could keep him from behind the wheel of his hideously battered old pickup, though. It was his practice to rove the hill roads from daylight till long after dark, inching along in low gear on whichever side of the road took his fancy.

Bump never gave ground to man, beast or logging truck. Never noticed them. He was almost stone deaf, too. Many a driver had come head-on with Bump's pickup and been left stranded to hike home. Bump would just back away from a collision, pull around the obstacle and drive on, heedless of dragging bumper, broken headlight, rubbing fender or flat tire. His victims never even got a "Howdy."

My grandfather, Poppy, was a typical Ozark rabbit hunter. That is to say, he reduced it to a leisurely sport, almost drawing-room in character. That's why he needed so many kids.

Poppy would take his stand on a stump or solid brush pile. He would send the kids out to beat the brush, forcing their way through tangles of wild grape vines, briars, buckbrush and thistles. They would stomp and scream, driving the rabbits into range of Poppy's shotgun.

When one patch was worked out, Poppy would saunter to

the next. Any kid caught in a brush pile, which happened frequently, was left to extricate himself, like Bump Crowder's victims.

"Nothing relaxes a man like a rabbit hunt," Poppy would say that evening.

The kids, scratched and bleeding, noses running and ears frostbitten, would be lying in exhausted heaps around the stove. They'd doze off, whimper and jerk around in their slumber like an old dog hunting in its dreams.

Poppy believed that rabbit hunting spoiled a good dog.

The best thing about riding a school bus was getting off in the afternoon and walking the half-mile home. The browsing was especially good in the fall.

Wild grapes were a staple. They grew everywhere—along the fence rows, in trees, over old buildings. If they escaped loggers and fires in the woods, vines grew as thick as a man's thigh. The grapes hang on most of the winter.

Most common variety was a small one we called possum grapes—sour with a thick skin and more seeds than pulp. A bunch of them stayed the appetite and quenched the thirst. No doubt the coat of dust deposited by passing vehicles provided necessary minerals, too.

Another and rarer type was sweet and nearly as large as a Concord. My grandfather told me this variety was the "genuine, old-time wild grape" and that its vines blanketed the county before "furriners" moved in. The furriners probably brought possum grapes from St. Louis, I calculated.

In the hollow behind Dripping Spring Church was a grove of persimmon trees where the gorgeous golden fruits would ripen after the first frost. Persimmons were cloying sweet and sticky, but after a few bites you could wash and get a drink at the spring. Then you could poke around fallen tree trunks and into holes to see how many possums you could scare up. Possums came in droves when the persimmons ripened. They ate at night and slept all day.

We used to pack persimmons in cotton wool and mail them as gifts. Made a fine present, grandfather said. "Shows we're thinking of them and it's nothing you'd want to eat yourself."

Hickory nuts drop from trees in the fall if there are any left up there. Squirrels build condominiums near hickory groves and they usually harvest direct from the tree. We didn't mind very much. Hickory nuts take a lot of work for little reward.

Besides, there were black walnuts—big as your fist in their green-black hulls that blackened everything they touched. The thing to do was to put the walnuts in gunny sacks, carry them home and spread them to dry. Then you would fill a gunny sack about halfway and put it outside the kitchen door for people to wipe their feet on. If you had a lot of company, you could hull half a sack of walnuts in no time at all, and with no effort.

Even then farmers were touchy about their black walnut trees. They'd put the dogs on a stranger messing around. Slickers were always coming through and buying the trees with phony checks. Later they turned to unadorned rustling, sawing the trees down and hauling them off.

Wild turkeys roosted in the woods between Dripping Spring and John's house. You'd see them running like sneaks, seldom flying. When John wanted turkey he turned his cattle into the woods for several nights. The turkeys would become used to the animals and to the bell of the lead cow. Then one evening John would walk into the woods with the herd, carrying the cowbell, right up to the roosting tree, and shoot one or two.

I once told John that friends of mine drive hundreds of miles, climb mountains in the dark and lie in cover imitating the wild turkey's mating call to get a shot at one of the birds. Often they fail.

"Mercy," John said, vastly amused.

Nowadays the hill people butcher hogs any time of the year. Just load one in the pickup and haul it to the locker plant. It comes home a few days later wrapped in white paper for the freezer.

But amenities like locker plants and freezers weren't widely available until after World War II. Up till the late 1940s there was a hog-killing season in the hills, late fall and early winter. That's when you made most of your meat for the year. It was a time of high feasting. Then you stretched the rest of the meat out the rest of the year.

Often two or three families got together to share the work, the necessary equipment and the meat. Sometimes they hired a skilled butcher. Clive Young was one of the best in the Eleven Points River country.

Clive was a recluse's recluse. He lived for 25 or 30 years in a tent in the woods. He was a squatter, by permission if necessary, but he preferred to move by stealth. Lived in Old Man Burns's woods for two winters before they noticed him. When the Burnses started poking around, Clive moved out in a huff.

He kept a pack of dogs and some goats. Cold nights he'd let more animals inside the tent. Most of the year Clive cut railroad ties, shaping them with an axe. Handmade ties last several times as long as those cut by saws. Why, I can't say.

If you're going to butcher a hog, you have to catch it first. People might keep brood sows, weaner and feeder pigs in pens. They were a cash crop, not for butchering. The others ranged the woods, fattening in the fall on acorns. They were wild animals. Some eluded capture for years, particularly during the war when many hill farms were abandoned.

Few things are more frightening or more determined than an angry hog. About the only thing that will turn one from a charge is a good hog dog clamped on one ear. There is no such thing as a bad hog dog. The first mistake is fatal. If you decide to hunt hogs, get yourself a Platt hound, an old one.

When you've penned your hogs, feed them corn for a week or two to take the rank taste out of the meat and add some fat. Then set a date and get your equipment ready.

You'll need two barrels for scalding, enough big old iron kettles for rendering lard, more skillets than you would believe, grinders, spices, a tree with a sturdy limb the right height for your block and tackle and lots of dry kindling wood. Better cut more wood.

When the hog was killed, it would be hoisted into the air and Clive would slash it open from "geezle to tail." Then it would be dipped into a barrel of boiling water to loosen the bristles. While others were scraping the bristles off, Clive would separate liver and other edible innards from the offal.

Boiling water and precise timing is needed to loosen the bristles. If you scald the carcass too long, something bad happens, though I can't remember what. Hill people still congratulate each other on a neat bit of work or clever remark by saying, "You got a good scald on that 'un."

Clive would reduce a scraped carcass to its various parts in a very few minutes. Fat went into the rendering kettles and the resultant lard into crocks or five-gallon cans. Hams, bacon and sidemeat (sorry stuff but there was lots of it) were set aside for the smokehouse. There were stacks of spareribs and backbones.

Most of the rest was ground into sausage—loins and all. There was so much fresh meat that had to be eaten in a hurry that roasts, chops and cutlets were a rarity. They were ground up.

Sausage-making was an art. No two recipes were alike. Women traded recipes often, but they always kept something back. A woman would sample sausage made from her recipe and exclaim, "Mercy, don't seem just right. But I can't think why." She knew why, all right.

Sausage was fried immediately and preserved in jars in its own grease. Some people fried chunks of pork and kept them that way, too.

His work done, Clive would collect his pay, including a modest portion of the meat, and disappear into the woods. For the next few days the people he left behind would feast on fresh pork, eating until their ears stuck straight out.

It was not uncommon to hear that a whole family was "off its feet" from overindulgence. But it only happened once a year.

The tag-end of winter in the Ozarks can be a time of perpetual rain. There will be weeks of fog and mist and drizzle. And every so often the clouds will settle in and do a real job of it. This time it got serious about raining on Thursday night, stuck to it through Friday and when the alarm went off at 4:30 Saturday morning, it was still coming down with a steady beat.

By the time Pop and my sister and I gathered in the kitchen, the dogs, Queenie and her pup, Ring, had returned to the back porch. The cows were in the cane field, half a mile from the barn, and the gulley and meadow in between were covered with water, a torrent 200 yards wide. This sort of thing wasn't covered in a stock dog's basic labor agreement. Queenie wanted instructions.

Pop told me to take Dan, our grumpy old horse of all trades, and get the cows. The current was fast enough to make it real work and Dan had to swim hard. It didn't improve his temper. The cows took to the water easily since there was feed waiting in the barn. They strung out in the water just like in a John Wayne movie. I enjoyed the whole thing until I dismounted to lead Dan back to his stall. He bit me on the seat hard enough to raise blood blisters.

The cows came into the milking parlor in regular order, which they set themselves. Boss animals first, then right down through the ranks to Spook, a neurotic Jersey that couldn't whip anything in the lot. Milking cold, wet cows is no treat. They eat fast and then fidget. A wet cow tail weighs about 10 pounds and when one of them works from a full windup, she can bring tears to your eyes. Cows also have a knack for swatting you just as you open your mouth.

When Spook had been milked, Pop poured some for the barn cats in an old chick feeder. The calico cat had a litter of kittens and Brigham, the tomcat, had honored us with his presence. Brigham caught his own food, rabbits, quail, squirrels and the like, but he always took a few ritual laps of the milk—first and alone. The old females pretended to ignore the milk until Brigham had finished. The kittens sat in a line, quivering, until Brigham had stepped back. Then they rushed for places. It only took one swat from Brigham to teach a new kitten manners.

Pop and I drove three miles with our cans of milk to Osa Davidson's. Osa would take them on to town. En route we saw old Bump Crowder's pickup halfway down a hillside and wedged in a thicket of saplings. Tracks showed that Bump had slid off the road and tried every whichaway to get back on it. The whole hillside was torn up. A tank battle wouldn't have left more sign. "Bump is a hard man to convince," Pop remarked.

Back home for breakfast, we strung our wet denim jumpers above the kitchen stove and put our shoes on the oven door. Then we contemplated the possibilities of a rainy Saturday.

"We could grind some hay," Pop said. I slid off my chair and lay flat on the floor under the kitchen table. "I think it's my heart," I said. Pop laughed and tabled the motion. It was our practice to grind hay in a hammermill, which is just what it sounds like, and mix it with regular dairy feed. That cut down on waste. Grinding hay in the best of conditions, out in the open where you can breathe, is miserable work. Shut up in a barn it would be worse. Besides, we had plenty already ground. "Let's just spend the day wishing we had saved our summer wages," Pop said. "Wish in one hand and let it rain in the other. Let me know which one gets full first."

I got my favorite book, "Destry Rides Again," and lay sideways in the armchair in the front room. I almost knew it by heart and could read it in an hour, faster if I didn't choke up at the part where Destry's great mare, Fiddle, is finally worn down in a chase and the posse captures Destry because he won't let Fiddle break her heart trying to carry him to safety.

In the end it comes out all right. Destry didn't steal the payroll at all. It was the banker himself. The greatest disappointment of my young life was seeing the movie of the same name. They didn't keep anything but the title.

My sister got out the catalog, a tablet and a pencil. She started on Page 1 and made three lists—things she absolutely had to have before she started high school next fall, things she would buy immediately when she got rich and things she would buy for her friends if she got real rich. On that happy day, she announced, Mom would get a sewing machine, a lazy susan to hold spices and condiments and a musical powderbox that played "Londonderry Air." I didn't make the list.

Pop had gone to the barn to tinker. He liked to keep his hands busy. Mom was doing whatever mothers do. You don't notice them until you need them. Suddenly an aroma from the kitchen convinced me that I really needed her. She was making fried pies!

Fried pies have two special things going for them: They come off the griddle faster than you can eat them, and making them is hypnotic. Once she gets going, a proper mother will hardly ever stop making them until she has a gorgeous surplus. A fellow who always wondered whether he could eat 15 fried pies can find out on a rainy Saturday. He'll discover that he can't. Nobody can except Johnny Tapp.

My sister was standing on a footstool and Mom was pinning up the hem of a dress for her when Johnny rode up on his little brown mustang. Pop saw him coming and returned from the barn. Mom returned to her mixing bowl and griddle. There were only a couple of dozen pies left and we'd need plenty more.

Johnny was built like an oak stump and his appetite was legendary. Breakfast for Johnny started with fruit, a quart of it. Then he would have hot cereal and cold cereal. Then eggs, anywhere from six to 10, sausage, bacon, ham, cold meat or chicken left from the night before, biscuits beyond number with jam, milk and quarts of coffee strong enough to float a horseshoe.

While he ate fried pies, Johnny related the news. The roads to Olden, Pomona, White Church and Peace Valley were impassable. Bump Crowder was back at his pickup with a team of horses but wasn't likely to pull it out this day. The horses were slipping and falling and Bump was red as a turkey gobbler when Johnny rode past.

The new people down past Clyde Eubanks's had built a milking barn just across the road from their house. Johnny had advised against it, remarking mildly that he had often had to swim a horse across that spot. There was four feet of water running through the new barn, Johnny reported.

He had seen smoke coming from the summer kitchen of

another neighbor's house. When weather kept them indoors, that couple tended to fuss. Sooner or later one of them would move to the summer kitchen to wait for the sun to break through. Clive Young, the woodcutter, had left his tent in the woods and moved in with Jim Brotherton. Clive hadn't spoken a word to anyone in three or four years and Jim talked a blue streak. To his horses when there was no other audience. But Jim never required answers. He and Clive got along fine.

Johnny had enough news to keep us occupied until evening milking. As we walked to the barn, it was still raining hard.

"You think it will ever stop?" I asked.

"Well," Pop said, "it always has."

A writer for one of the eastern magazines took a run down home and reported that brush arbor revivals are coming back. That's interesting, if not completely accurate. They've never been away.

There's been at least one every summer in the Eleven Points country for as long as Grandma Bandy can remember. And she remembers the year the preacher's daughter swallowed a tadpole or snake or something slimy during a mass running-water immersion at Jack's Fork and left the country with an itinerant water dowser, saying that she had enjoyed as much country religion as she could stand for the time being.

That has been a while, but aside from the fact that people come in pickups and dusty cars instead of wagons, brush arbor revivals haven't changed much. Drive across country instead of encapsulating yourself on a freeway and you'll find them near places like Three Brothers, Ark., and Duck

River Suck, Ala., and such backwaters as Houston, Texas, and Miami, Fla.

What happens is that a like-minded group finds a suitable field. They cut the brush and pile it tremendously high in amphitheater shape. Then they build plank seats out front and at the end of each row place a lantern or a torch. Bundles of cattails soaked in kerosene and crankcase oil make good torches. They burn forever and the smoke keeps off some of the bugs. Nowadays you can set up a generator and use electric lights, but torches add something.

You have a speaker. Not always, but usually it is someone from far away, tinged with the glamor of distant triumphs. Quite often a local preacher will serve as a sponsor. Those who are saved will need a shepherd when the traveling preacher moves on after a week.

Almost always there will be a singer, a woman or young girl with long hair that shimmers in the torchlight. She'll wear a white robe and probably play an instrument, too, the silver cornet, perhaps. There will be other singers, local as a rule, and a portable organ.

Songs and music and the preacher's voice will bounce off that brush arbor and echo for miles through the hills.

The preacher is the main thing. He'll dress soberly, conser-

vatively, but with a flair, a distinctive touch like a long black coat. He'll be a scholar usually, a student of the scriptures and of other things. He'll let you know it and use a few big words as evidence. But mostly he'll talk so you can understand.

He'll tell you that you may be troubled and lonely, but that you're not alone. He'll talk of faraway places and of the people there, people like you. He'll pound that point home and his listeners will light up. They'll laugh and sing and shout sometimes. They'll turn sober and thoughtful when something strikes home.

The preacher will put on a show. He'll work the standard themes, the scarlet women in silken gowns, the brown ruin that is unleashed when a whisky bottle is uncapped. He'll talk of men who yield to temptation while a good woman and wee ones wait at home. Of women who take to painting their faces and hanging out in honkytonks.

Mostly though, he'll talk of the simple virtues. Honesty, decency, fairness.

For a week there will be drama, excitement and tension. Talk will run around the community each morning of those who were "saved" the previous evening. Those are the ones who come forward for the preacher's blessing. Many are sobbing. Some of them "testify." They talk of what has been troubling them, of deeds and thoughts they regret. Lay down your burden, the preacher will say, and start fresh.

Mid-July in the Ozarks and the hay crop is made. Spring rains were good and the barn is stuffed. Oat hay first, then sweet clover. Then the fragrant mixture from the big meadow, lespedeza, yellow bud, red top, timothy and red clover.

Not a forkful got wet, either. It turned dry at cutting time and now, three weeks later, hasn't rained a drop . The rain frogs tried to holler up a storm several times but no luck. A little dew on the grass this Sunday morning, so there'll be no rain today, either. It is a sign that seldom fails. If there is no dew, look for a shower.

And it is hot. Oppressive. Not a breath of air. The night before you kicked off the sheet and lay awake listening to the whippoorwills. Heard your father get up twice, go to the kitchen for a dipper of water to sprinkle on the sheets. It only helps for a few seconds.

The alarm clicks at 4:30, preparatory to ringing, and Pop's hand hits the button on top to stop it. His feet hit the floor and it is milking time. Queenie, the stock dog, and her pup Ring start after the cows without command as soon as they hear Pop.

The cows are pasturing on sudan grass, a sweet, canelike, hot-weather grass higher than their backs. They won't want to come in. Too full and too hot. No feed for them either, just a handful to coax their heads into the stanchions.

"Like to see it come a real gulley-washer," Pop says as we walk to the barn, kicking the grass moodily. "Like to step on a $10 bill instead of cowpiles, too."

"What would you spend it on, Pop?"

"Warm socks and a winter jacket."

"Not me. Twenty gallons of ice cream. Eat all I could and go swimming in the rest."

"You'll die poor," says Pop, "but too happy to care."

Back at the house after milking, the kitchen is like a furnace. My mother has breakfast ready. And noon dinner. And supper. Sausage, fried eggs, biscuits, enormous bowls of wild blackberries picked the day before, whole mess of fried chicken, blackberry cobbler just coming out of the oven.

"The cook is through work for the day," she says. "Maybe till it rains. Pick what you want, but remember it's got to last till bedtime."

Paper fans from the Mountain View funeral parlor get a workout at church. There aren't enough to go around. Lots of dotted swiss dresses on the girls, sticking to them here and there. Every so often, you see a girl pull her bodice loose and blow down on her chest. Look too intently and your mother's elbow digs into your ribs. "What?" you ask in an indignant whisper. "You know what," she whispers back and digs you again.

Home from church, Pop throws some gunny sacks in the back of the truck and tells you to come along. Eight miles to town and the ice plant. "Better make it three blocks," Pop tells the man. That is 75 pounds, but it melts fast even wrapped in sacks.

Swing into the neighbor's place. Johnny and Letha are on the porch, rocking and fanning. "Might be worth the drive down this evening," Pop says, gesturing toward the ice. "Evening" in the Ozarks is anytime past noon. "Might do that," says Johnny.

Letha did her cooking early, too. They bring more chicken and biscuits, a bowl of sliced tomatoes, onions and cucumbers in vinegar-and-sugar dressing, a smoked turkey from Johnny's smokehouse, hickory-and-salt to the tongue.

Break up ice for the hand-cranked ice cream freezer, put the big chunks in a sack and pound them with the flat side of a pole axe. "Careful with the salt," Johnny warns. "Don't want it to run in the cream." Most of the natives call it "cream," not ice cream. Turning the crank is a boy's job, endless. Pop checks every now and then to see if it's thickening, then takes over to open the freezer. Magic! It's ready. Two gallons go in minutes.

Pudd Wallis and his wife Soula Belle drive past. Going to supper in town at their married daughter's. Her husband is a foreman at the sawmill now. He was a wild young man.

"Everybody thought he'd turn out sorry," Pop says. "Goes to show."

Pudd won't have a tractor on his place. "I'm a horse lover," he always says. "Time Pudd gets around and gets his team up and gets out to the fields," says Johnny, "there ain't enough of the day left to put a strain on a man."

Dogs flop in the dust under the porch, kids on the grass under the catalpa trees, old folks sit on the porch. Soon it's milking time again. "I might be willing to do a boy's chores for him," Johnny says, "if I knowed he was up here turning a freezer handle while I was milking."

Workwise, it's a poor trade, but Pop likes the idea. He and Johnny go to the barn while you break up some more ice. There's just enough left.

Afterward, in the dusk, there's more ice cream, cobbler, pieces of chicken like backs, necks, wings that you'd passed over earlier.

Johnny gets to talking, as he does about once a year. He takes you from the year the old bull got his daddy, to running wild horses with his brothers and an uncle out in Texas, to standing guard at Fort Carson during the war, to the tornado that lifted his old house right up off his head as he and Letha and their boy crouched in the fruit cellar.

The whippoorwills start calling again and Johnny and Letha prepare to go home. "Mercy, don't you wash them dishes," says Letha. "I'll take them home dirty." Mother lets it go that way. "Too hot to argue," she says.

"I wish it would come a real frog-drowner," says Johnny, as he leaves.

———————————

The layered look, which makes it possible for one to be both stylish and warm, is relatively new in high fashion. Shoot, most everybody in the Eleven Points country grew up stylish. We just didn't know it, probably because Capper's Weekly devoted most of its attention to new ways to embroider feedsacks.

A few words about feedsacks. Farm women made curtains, dresses, towels, sheets, slipcovers, pillowcases, men's underpants and maybe even what my grandfather called "unmentionables" from them.

The biggest development in what we now call agribusiness in my time was the introduction of patterned feedsacks. Before that the sacks were either burlap or white cotton, which could be used for sewing.

Women in our part of the country kept the Rit dye people solvent. Some interesting effects were achieved and a neighbor of ours who had a tendency to moon over her dyepot may actually have invented tie-dyeing. When a batch of sacks turned out too funny to display, she would make underpants for her son, Laidlaw. Old Laidlaw was the talk of the locker room at school.

Then came the patterned sacks. The privately owned mill in town was the first to get them, charging a nickel more than for plain. Made no difference. The mill boss would set up a line of sacks on the dock, displaying every pattern offered. Women from all over the Eleven Points country would walk up and down the line telling their husbands they wanted six of this and four of that.

The manager of the Farmers Exchange held out for a while. He had a duty to his members to keep costs down, he said. But it soon became apparent that without the fancy sacks, there wouldn't be any feed business to worry about.

Inevitably, there was profiteering. When sales of a particular pattern took off, the boss of the private mill would switch it to a more expensive line of feed. A dairy farmer who came to town with orders to get enough yellow-checked sacks to finish a set of curtains or dress a daughter would discover that yellow checks came only with high-protein feed.

This caused some hard feelings. It left a man between a rock and a hard place. If he pleased his ladies, he also was giving his cows a taste of high living and the critters would sulk and stomp for a few days when he switched them back to the old feed.

Now back to the layered look.

Every farm kitchen I was ever in had a long row of hooks or nails on one wall. In summertime they held straw hats, paper fans and flyswatters. Come cold weather they were loaded with the foul-weather gear.

One hook always looked like a display photo from the Monkey Wards catalog: New denim jumper, warm heavy coat, plaid hat with earflaps—and on the floor below, a new pair of black rubber boots. The gear on this hook belonged to the head of the house. He bought new.

The rest of the family wore his castoffs along with the debris of generations. The hooks in Charlie Burns's kitchen, for instance, held a World War I army overcoat, sweaters that his mother had knitted, bib overalls whose legs had worn off up to the knees. You could almost tell how long a family had farmed a place by checking the hooks. Boots under the secondary hooks usually bore red and yellow tire patches.

One virtue of denim jumpers and overalls is that they wear from the edges, the cuffs of sleeves and legs. Thus a jumper can serve generations, with each year's frazzle trimmed from the cuffs. It may begin service covering a man with a 48-inch chest and eventually become the property of a 10-year-old boy. But by that time, the sleeves have worn off to the original elbows.

The boy can fill out the body by first donning three sweaters, carefully chosen so that their holes don't match. Over everything he can pull a vast pair of bib overalls, cinching them at the waist with an old belt or a piece of rope. Don't use baling wire. Eventually an end will work through everything and stab you.

It is important to cinch tight. My sister's belt parted one morning and she slipped on the ice. She lay helpless and squawling about six inches off the ground. She was wearing several sweaters, two jumpers and the remnants of a sheepskin coat and the whole caboodle had slid around behind.

Great care also is necessary in selecting socks. One with a hole in the toe should be covered by another with a hole in the heel. None of the articles I have read on the layered look mention this. But then, I suppose fashion models don't spend a lot of time slopping hogs in patched boots.

4/Carry me to town

Summer evenings when I was a teen-ager slid together like beads on a string or like simple, pleasant piano music, variations on a theme. When it ended, the summer was a single piece of art. Touch one bead and the whole string would glimmer again in memory. Play a few notes and other parts of the composition would come to mind . . . a face, a party, the big pool game, diving off the high rock at Jack's Fork. . . .

At dusk when chores were done and supper eaten, boys would dress carefully. We wore shiny brown pleated gabardine slacks, argyle socks, brown loafers and usually a freshly ironed white shirt, open at the throat and turned back twice at the wrists. Sleeves were never buttoned, never rolled.

Boys run in packs of three for social purposes as a rule. (When you see more of them, they've organized for some purpose.) One of the three would have the use of a car or pickup. The boy who got transportation would send word: "Be ready, I'll carry you to town." We'd drive the dirt and gravel roads to town, along the ridges and swooping down to cross what hillbilly imitators called "cricks" and we called "branches."

Our town offered girls to look at—wearing penny loafers and ankle bracelets—and the Business Men's Club, a pool hall where the town sports would shoot rotation for as high as a dollar a game and advise us on life. ("Why keep a cow when milk's so cheap?") There was the Cinderella Confectionery, where you could get pop or ice cream or any kind of food that could be fried. We loved the town although we

affected not to and often talked of getting out to "civilization" after graduation. That meant Peoria for most of us, where the Caterpillar plant hired a good percentage of each senior class.

Life in town flowed around the square. The courthouse was in the middle and the four principal streets ended at the square. Everyone in town was bound to pass through several times a day. The sages roosted there and passed judgment.

Young people congregated there. The young bucks, slicked up after a day's work, used to park on the side nearest the Business Men's Club. They would sit on the shiny hoods of their cars, eye the girls who promenaded in clusters of summery color around and around the square, and celebrate their manhood.

"Hey, boy, what'd I hear about you and that Collins girl?" one would surely shout at a new arrival.

"What you mean? You ain't heard nothin'," the accosted one would reply in mock outrage and secret delight.

The others would take it up. "Better look out, lotta woman there." Or "That gal, will turn you ever' way but loose, buddy." That would go on till the first show started at the movie house.

Joe Green's drugstore was up the street from the pool hall. The high school crowd hung out there. Romances blossomed and died there. Joe healed many a broken heart with his cherry Cokes. He had dope for pimples. And if you had a sore throat, he'd paint it with some vile mixture, charge you a quarter. Embarrassed adolescent boys would stand for minutes, ignoring the two clerks, waiting to catch Joe's eye. He'd stroll back to his prescription counter and certain intimate commodities would be dispensed.

The sages saw it all, forgot nothing, talked it over the next day. They were always around the square, some of them. They worked there or owned businesses or loafed there.

And they knew. If a woman shopped there, they knew within minutes what for and how much. They'd match it with her husband's income, their house payments, the amount due on the overhaul of their car—all common knowledge.

The sages would log customers at Eli's liquor store, half a block off the square, and at the bus depot. When a merchant took to driving to Springfield on Friday afternoons and a woman who worked in a county office started catching the 4 o'clock bus, the sages knew what was going on.

One of the sages was a sleepless enforcer of her own moral code. The summer that "The Outlaw," a movie featuring Jane Russell's chest, played in Willow Springs, 19 miles away, she wore out a set of tires.

The film was flat banned in our town, largely through her efforts. The theater at Willow Springs was supposed to limit admissions to 18-year-olds or over, but anybody's money was good there.

This lady drove up every evening and watched for kids from our town. Then she would phone their parents. The parents would call the Willow Springs night marshal, or drive up themselves and drag their offspring from the theater.

In our town, the first show let out at 10 o'clock and by 10:30

the square was dark and quiet except for the Cinderella Confectionery, where you could listen to Hank Williams on the jukebox.

But this lady, the enforcer, hung on. She would sit in her car watching for couples. Then she would follow them at a discreet distance. She knew every parking place in the county, could deduce where they were heading almost as soon as they decided. After a fiendishly calculated interval, she would drive slowly past the parked car, headlights on high beam. The couple would be left wondering whether she would talk. She would.

For serious sinning there were only two possibilities in our town. Motels, actually old rat-traps of the sort once called cabin camps. When a couple checked in, the lady would call the spouses or parents of each and the police. There were laws governing cohabitation, fornication and adultery and she saw to it that they were vigorously enforced.

That lady testified at a lot of trials and divorce cases. "I just happened to be passing . . ." her testimony invariably began.

A few years ago she failed her eye test and lost her driving license. The local paper carried an item and sold every copy in half an hour. Everybody in town knew someone they wanted to send a clipping to.

People my age are always saying, "Every Saturday, we'd go" to the Gem or the Isis or the Odeon or whatever movie house. But it wasn't that often. Once a month, twice at most. Everything had to work just right.

Money for one. A dime admission and a nickel or dime to spend. Weather. "If the creek don't rise" was stipulated, meaning anything unfavorable. It might be haying weather.

Nothing interferes with that.

The folks had to adjust their schedule, wait around after they finished their trading. A double feature, cartoon and serial likely meant late milking and a cold, scratch supper.

You wore your "good pants," bought baggy and kept for best until they were skin-tight and wouldn't button. Mother would let them out once. Dangerous, that. Yelled once during a George O'Brien western and everything went. Buttons popped 10 feet and the back seam split all the way.

I slid out of the theater with my back to the wall, hid in the restroom until the show was over, then slid outside. Pop was parked up the street. He kept honking and beckoning; I kept waving for him to drive down to me so I could dash to the car. He finally did it. Maddest I ever saw him. Then he laughed all the way home.

My movie was the Avenue, maybe the crumbiest theater in the world. They opened it only on Saturdays, to save wear and tear on the good one up the street. No adult ever ventured into the Avenue. It was narrow, about eight seats to the row. The seats were wooden and all broken. You eased down gently or the cracks would grab a hunk of meat.

Old Man Brown ran the Avenue. His daughter sold tickets and another relative ran the popcorn machine and sold caramel-covered apples, a big item for a reason that will become apparent. Brown stood at the entrance and frisked us. We liked to smuggle in apples, pears and green peaches, but seldom got away with it. Brown would grab a handful of hair and make us shuck out our pockets.

We had favorite seats. Bully Comstock and his crowd always took the second row. That way they could put their feet up on the first-row seats or patrons and still be in the thick of the action. Bully was big for his age and he was quite a bit older than the rest of us. Spent four years in the fourth grade. He was determined to get a high school diploma, which he did at about age 23. His grandfather promised to leave Bully the farm if he made it. Old Man Brown never messed with Bully.

The Avenue stood between a vacant building and the town's largest mercantile establishment, a general store that sold everything and bought almost anything—hides, cream, eggs, nuts, fruit. Rats lived in the vacant building and did their grocery shopping in the back of the store. The shortest route was across the stage of the Avenue.

Two or three times during a Saturday movie, a hungry rat would scamper across the stage, throwing a huge, hump-backed shadow on the screen. That's when the caramel apples and any ammunition we'd smuggled in came in handy. We'd cut loose. That's why Bully sat up front. He had the best shot.

Everybody in the county claims they saw it, but I was actually there on the Big Day. It happened during the serial. I don't remember the title, but this evil mastermind had thrown the hero and the girl who was rightfully entitled to the fortune her grandfather had left her a map to into a dungeon. (Sort that sentence out yourself; that's the story line.) The evil mastermind was letting in water. "Gonna drownd 'em!" somebody shouted.

A rat started across the stage. Halfway across, befuddled by the apples and such coming at it, the rat doubled back and then began whirling around like a dog chasing its tail.

Bully leaped to his feet, roaring, taking aim for a killing shot. Somebody zinged a caramel apple, half-licked, stick and all, from way back. It hit Bully and stuck in his hair. He whirled and was hit by half a dozen more.

Bully went wild. He raised one size-15 foot and smashed down the seat behind him. The whole row collapsed, being bolted together. It caught the legs of the kids in the next row, trapping them.

Bully whacked everybody within reach, raised his other foot and stomped down the next row. Bellowing, raging, stomping, he worked his way back through the theater, flattening every row. That apple was stuck tight in his hair, flopping and wriggling. Kids screaming and crying. Old Man Brown blowing his police whistle. (I forgot to mention that earlier.)

When I got outside, Old Man Brown was out in the street, blowing his whistle. That was the Avenue's Big Day. Modern theater has known few such moments.

———————————

I can't remember which year it was that we had two Thanksgivings—God's and Roosevelt's. I know it was the year my Aunt Anna read that Tom Dewey's favorite snack was an onion sandwich and immediately switched to the Democratic Party.

Uncle Bill blew his cork. He believed that the man who had broken up Murder Incorporated was going to save the Republican Party some day. "Look at the man's record!" he shouted at Anna. "Look at his qualifications!" Anna replied that she didn't want to look at the stinky little thing. However, the onion-sandwich controversy, the third-term issue and Adolf Hitler were all put aside for a while. We had a more important matter to deal with.

The way it began, Roosevelt issued a proclamation to the effect that Thanksgiving would come a week early.

Our Republican newspaper said that this was just typical of the arrogant Godlessness of that man in the White House.

Our Democrat newspaper asked whether we wanted to wallow in a lot of cheap emotionalism or get the economy rolling. For Roosevelt's purpose, though he may not have stated it baldly, was to ensure a longer Christmas shopping season.

Well, there you have it: God versus mammon. Our national heritage was being desecrated, the Republican editor claimed. Our Democrat editor called the opposition the self-appointed Sons of the Founding Fathers and said the original Pilgrims picked the date out of one of their funny hats.

The community took up sides. Almost immediately it became clear that there would be two Thanksgivings, God's and Roosevelt's, and you had to pick one.

Merchants, although about 98 percent Republican politically, met every night for a week trying to reach accord. They never did. Some closed one day, some another. The garage where my father worked closed both days, but the men were paid only for one holiday. Pop was a Roosevelt man and he decided that he wanted his full week's pay for the president's week. Some of the mechanics were Republicans and they took the pay cut the first week so they could blame it on Roosevelt.

We kids defended our fathers' positions lustily. By early November we were dividing up for noontime games as the Roosevelts and the Pilgrims.

It was decided that school would close both days. That didn't satisfy anybody. We gave our Thanksgiving pageant twice, though our paper Pilgrim hats and Indian feathers looked pretty droopy the second time around. Some mothers came the first time, the rest the second week.

A preacher who called himself the Rocky Mountain Mauler from Rocky Ford (he was a boxer before he heard the call) tried to organize a campaign to physically open the school for a prayer service on Roosevelt's Thanksgiving.

It was mother's turn to invite the relatives. She asked them for Roosevelt's day. Aunt Anna accepted. Uncle Bill said he would come but wouldn't eat with us. Anna said he could have an onion sandwich in the back yard.

On Roosevelt's day we dressed up and feasted. Kids who were eating normally roamed around the community jeering at the Roosevelts. The next week we did the same to the Pilgrims.

My father went into politics with high ideals and secret misgivings. My Uncle Lurvy warned him that the life of a public servant was grim and thankless.

Lurvy had served as road commissioner of the township that adjoined our village. What a road commissioner did in those days, the early 1930s, was drive a motor grader, smoothing out the township's dirt roads.

He got $4 a day for eight or 10 days' work a month. Good money, but he had to maintain the grader. The one the township owned was a sorry wreck. Even Lurvy, who was a genius with heavy machinery, finally had to give up on it.

He hitched four horses to it one day, pulled it through the woods to an abandoned lead mine and rolled it over the edge. It sank in 50 feet of water.

Then Lurvy went to a highway project several counties away and sort of borrowed a motor grader. He drove it home in two nights, laying up in the woods through the daylight hours. Technically you could claim that Lurvy stole that motor grader. But he always intended to return it, he said, as soon as the township bought itself a new one.

Things went well for a couple of years. Then some part broke or wore out and Lurvy couldn't repair it. He had to order one. When the order with its serial numbers reached the Caterpillar factory in Peoria, some long-nosed book-keeper started hollering for the law.

Township officeholders, who had been bragging up their road program and asking no questions, expressed shock. They said they'd just assumed Lurvy had slapped a coat of paint on the old scraper; that is, if they thought of it at all. There was talk of doing something drastic to Lurvy, but nothing came of it. The president of the construction company that owned the grader thought it was funny and he had already collected insurance.

If anybody pressed charges, it would have to be the insurance company. Naturally that ended that. No insurance company ever won a case in front of an Ozark jury in those days. I doubt if one has yet.

The experience left Lurvy bitter. "The voters will turn on you at the first sign of trouble," he told my father.

Pop should have listened, but he didn't. He was part of the Reform Slate for Village Board. Their slogan was "Out of the Mud and into the Twentieth Century." The big issue was sidewalks. Pop's group thought the town should have one.

The business district was pretty well built up on both sides of the block, Pop's slate pointed out, but the high board-walks were unsightly and dangerous. Dogs and chickens and stray hogs were always sleeping under them and many of the boards were rotten. Some were missing. A woman who was what we called "fleshy" fell through in front of the grocery store one day and was trapped for 15 minutes. That was a good talking point. You couldn't expect to attract new investors, big money men from Kansas City, if their wives couldn't walk the streets.

The old gang of rascals who had run the village for 40 years favored replacing the missing and rotten boards gradually as finances permitted.

It was an era of liberalism, with President Roosevelt priming the pump, and the Reform Slate swept to victory.

For one glorious day. Then the old gang went to court, claiming election fraud. No voting booths, they said, the ballots weren't secret. That was true. Everybody just took a ballot at the door of the village hall and went off to one of the tables along the wall and marked it. The judge ordered a new election.

The old gang pulled out all the stops. The sawmill owner, one of the rascals, donated lumber to fix the boardwalks. The marshal patrolled the block several times a day, shooing away the livestock.

Now most people kept chickens and fattened a hog or two in a backyard pen, but there weren't any cows in town. People used canned milk mostly. There were two brands, Pet and Carnation. They tasted the same and cost the same, but for some reason, people who used one brand felt that those who bought the other were a little tacky.

Ours was a Carnation village by a big majority. My mother used Pet. Tacky. Then Old Man Dockery, who ran the store and was one of the old gang, raised the price of Pet two cents. Now the opposition had Mom both ways. She was tacky and putting on airs besides.

Then the dog license rumor swept the village. The Reform Slate was going to finance its highfalutin' improvements— and probably line its own pockets—by putting a tax on dogs.

By chance none of the Reform Slate kept dogs. Oh, maybe one or two pets, but no coon hounds, bird dogs, beagles for rabbits or feists for squirrels. But a dog tax would bankrupt pretty near every other household in town.

That did it. The voters panicked. The old gang was returned to office in a landslide.

The carnival that tried to "dee-foul our community and entice our youngsters"—a direct quote from an Eleven Points officeholder—picked the wrong time and the wrong place, let me tell you. Communists, most likely, everybody said after the dust settled.

But when they tried their nasty tricks at our county fair, they met their match. They ran into an informed citizenry, a crusading editor and an alert city government. Both of the latter, as it happened, were fresh from triumphs over international conspiracies.

We citizens were informed because our local editor had given the matter considerable thought and had concluded that the Communists and the International Jewish Conspiracy—actually the same outfit or closely aligned, as far as he was concerned—had selected the Eleven Points region as their first target for takeover of the nation. He could prove it. Hadn't the commies put Harry Truman in the White House? That showed what a power base they had in the Ozarks.

Our editor wrote a column. And on days when he wasn't snapping the whip at merchants who had cut back on their advertising budget, he kept us up to date on the Communist and Jewish menaces.

Just before the county fair opened, he had fought off a takeover of the local canning factory. He had fearlessly reported that "rumor hath it that two New York Jews" had bought the factory and were going to close it, ship all the berries out of town and beat down the price to practically nothing. If it weren't true, why hadn't the new owners taken out the usual half-page ad to announce opening dates and berry prices?

Well, the International Jewish Conspiracy capitulated overnight. Next day the ad appeared and the owners—whose names were Callahan and Murphy and who lived in St. Louis—announced that the factory would open as usual.

Just about this time, the Communists tried to organize the workers at the shoe factory. No doubt about it. They wanted to dictate hours and pay scales and drive the factory into bankruptcy, the manager said. If that wasn't communism, what was it?

Our editor and other forces for good swung into action, with the city council taking the lead. The council, learning that union organizers were meeting with workers one night, adjourned their own session and went en masse to the union meeting.

One councilman, who was pushing 80, ran down the center aisle of the meeting hall, shook his fists and shouted, "Fellow citizens, listen to me. Don't—." And he dropped dead right there. Never said don't what.

At the funeral everybody agreed that it was the way he would have wanted to go, fighting for freedom. The union organizers went back to Russia or wherever, though they did return and organize the factory several months later. Pushed wages up to 70 cents an hour in some departments.

Our editor said we should never relax our vigilance. If they were stopped one place, the Communists would try another. "Plug every rathole," he advised.

Sure enough, the next attempt was to undermine our morals. This carnival, which in addition to rides and games of skill provided the free stage show for the county fair, brought in "naked women flauntin' their bodies right out in the open air," according to an officeholder who had checked out the show three times the first day.

Fair attendance the next day set a record that may never be equalled. And the Dancing Sisters lived up to expectations.

Traditionally, the entertainment at our fair consisted of fiddlers in western outfits, one comical type in bib overalls who played the harmonica and maybe a lady singer. She wore a long dress and if she was young and pretty, might bounce or sway in time to the fast tunes. Kind of racy and we young sports would stomp and whistle.

But the Dancing Sisters—I forget their name—wore sequined costumes much like majorettes wear now. (Our majorettes wore skirts.) And the sisters tap-danced to hot numbers like "I Got Rhythm" right up there on the park bandstand with an accordion player.

I tell you, it was stimulating. Everybody was shocked. "See ever' thang they got," was the most common remark. "There'll be trouble," many said, and sure enough, there was.

On the third day the sisters wore skirts, short ones with several petticoats. But they were worse than the tight costumes. When they sashayed, the skirts swung up revealingly. By that time the local editor was thundering, preachers were up in arms and the sheriff was under great pressure to close the show before it totally corrupted the young people.

A kid named Freddie was the first casualty. Freddie was a 32nd-degree creep who spent all of his waking hours in the pool hall unless an Esther Williams movie was playing at the local theater. But naturally he turned out for the Dancing Sisters, taking position at the edge of the bandstand for each show and leaving a wet spot on its floor where he drooled. The accordion player got to know Freddie in a hurry and on the fourth evening, he edged over and stomped on his hand. Broke a finger, Freddie claimed.

Nobody really wanted to take up the cudgels in Freddie's

behalf, but that very night one of the leading watchdogs of community morals brought alarming news to the local police.

One of the Dancing Sisters, this woman said, had a man in her room at a cabin camp. The sheriff and I were playing pitch in the police station with the two night officers. We all went out.

Well, the dancer was tending a fussing baby and the man, the accordion player, had been cooking soup on a gas ring when the officers knocked. They said they were married and the sheriff would have left it there despite the local guardian of virtue if the accordion player hadn't got sore and shoved one policeman. They took the whole bunch down to the station and called the city attorney.

He was up for reelection and he knew an opportunity when he saw one. First he demanded to see their marriage certificate. They didn't have it. Then he asked for birth certificates. Didn't have those, either.

Couldn't even prove they were citizens. "That tells us something right there," the city attorney said. He and the local editor were close friends.

They made a deal. The Dancing Sisters and the accordion player left town that night. Next day, the carnival had fiddlers on the bandstand, a real decent act. And as far as I know, the Communists still haven't taken over the Eleven Points.

5/Neighbors

Sam Townsend set my feet on the path to self-confidence and taught me to use my elbows on the curves. I owe him.

Sam hired me as a chicken-plucker and garden-hoer the summer I was 10. Mostly, I think, he wanted an audience. He paid 10 cents a day, spot cash. This was not the invariable practice in our community. One woman paid me off for three days' work in pop bottles. I carried them to a store, which rejected many of them as being the wrong brand.

I was chubby, bashful, gullible and incredibly naive. My folks figured I would ask them if I wanted to know anything. I figured they would tell me.

Sam didn't set out to educate me. He just loved to talk and what I did best was listen. Sam's conversational voice was a confidential bellow. That summer he filled me in on local and county politics, the birth, background, current problems and likely prospects of anybody who drove by or came to Sam's mind and the general state of our tight little world. Sam's views were often startling and his language was explicit.

"Eula Mae's got the farm now and a potful of money," he might say as a newly widowed neighbor lady drove by. "Cuttin' a real rusty these days, but it won't last." And Sam would describe graphically just what "cuttin' a rusty" involved and with whom the widow was dallying. While I stood popeyed, Sam foretold how it would all end. Correctly, I should say.

"Am I right?" Sam would roar after delivering one of his pronouncements. "Damn right," he would answer himself.

I nursed a secret passion that summer. There was a lass named Anita. She had buck teeth, stringy blonde hair and a bewitching way of giggling and wiggling dirty brown toes that peeped from the holes in her tennis shoes. Somehow I must have betrayed my yearnings, for one morning a party of girls out picking berries perched on the fence by Sam's garden patch and serenaded me.

"Doctor, doctor, can you tell?" (they sang) "What will make Anita well. She is sick and about to die. And that would make poor Larry cry."

Anita was with them! She giggled and wiggled. I cringed and chopped several cucumber plants into salad sized hunks. I wanted to die.

Sam said nothing about the destruction of his cucumbers, but that afternoon as we plucked chickens, he told me a tale of his days "as a young buck in the merchant marine."

"This shipmate of mine come down with lockjaw every time he got close to a woman," Sam said. "Couldn't say boo. Some folks thought he was plain feeble, but that warn't so. Those women just warn't his style. He was partial to redheads. Let a redhead get into nuzzling distance and my shipmate would heat up like a depot stove."

Sam told about a wild night in Buenos Aires and his shipmate and a high-toned, handsome, redheaded woman and how Sam and his shipmate had to battle a knife-wielding husband and a whole gang to get back aboard ship.

Now Sam had never been south of Pocahontas, Ark., and he knew that I knew it. But Sam felt, and I agreed, that a man couldn't duck his responsibilities just because he wasn't in a specific place at a certain time. I knew Sam would have stuck with his shipmate. I'd have done the same thing.

I was greatly comforted by Sam's story of the shipmate who "warn't backward, just particular." At times I would wonder about the future and whether redheaded women would be my weakness. Anita was a forgotten fancy, the plaything of an idle hour.

Late that summer I had saved $4 in dimes and I blew the whole amount on a lunch pail, the largest one I had ever seen. My family was outraged. I didn't need a lunch pail, they told me. There were dozens of better ways to spend my savings. I was, in their opinion, a dope. But Sam didn't feel that way.

"Helluva lunch bucket you got there," Sam said. "Bet you could sleep all the Singer midgets in there." Then Sam told about a shipmate of his who bought a guitar. Couldn't play it. Didn't want to learn. Just wanted to look at it. "But a man's got a right to shoot his wad on anything that tickles his fancy," Sam said.

"Am I right?" he bellowed.

"Damn right," I whispered.

———————————————

Sam Townsend lived in luxurious squalor with his rooster, Hogan, named after a man Sam had sued unsuccessfully seven or eight times. Hogan the rooster had one eye, a bare bottom—feathers just wouldn't seem to stay on there—and walked with a limp. Hogan the man had lost an eye in World War I. He used a cane, and every time Sam spotted him on a trip to town he would holler, "Hogan, drop your pants. I want to check something out."

I spent a lot of time with Sam when I was 10 and 11 years old and to my way of thinking Sam was dead right when he boasted, "I got everything a man could want."

Sam spent his leisure hours in an armchair he claimed he bought from a house of ill repute in Pocahontas, Ark. Without leaving his chair, he could fry an egg on his wood range, let down the oven door to warm his feet or dry his shoes, turn on his radio or reach the valve trombone he was learning to play by the numbers. It was a revolutionary new system of teaching music, Sam said, developed by a Professor Doakes in St. Louis.

Hogan roosted on the woodpile beside the stove. In one corner was a pile of steel traps. Denim jumpers, heavy coats and wet-weather gear hung from nails. The walls were papered with front pages of newspapers, in case you wanted to read, and the house was as tight as tarpaper and hand-split hickory shakes could make it.

There were three other rooms, but Sam seldom went into them. No need. He slept by the stove on a cot and in hot weather he took it out on the back porch. Smoke from Sam's cob pipe and the smell of the hides he generally had tacked to the outside walls kept off the mosquitoes when he slept outside.

However, Sam lied when he said that he was content.

He suffered from the same urges that gripped Hogan in the spring when the pullets Sam raised reached a certain age. Matrimony was seldom far from Sam's mind.

Sam was a courtin' fool. One of the penalties of widowhood in the Eleven Points country was that Sam would come courtin' all fitted out in his blue serge suit and carrying a can of peach-flavored snuff in lieu of the homegrown twist he normally chewed. By the time I knew him Sam had already offered his hand to every maiden lady from Koshkonong to Three Brothers.

Finally Sam took to hiring housekeepers, hoping that propinquity would have an effect. That's all he did was hire them. They quit as soon as they saw Sam's house. Sam asked my mother for advice. She told him to shoot Hogan, throw away his trombone and burn the house.

Then to the astonishment of all of us, Miss Edith took the job. She was a maiden lady from down in the Arkansas rice country, about 50, slender and pleasant. We were all baffled, but she stayed on and on, for weeks. My mother visited and hinted that Sam wasn't every girl's dream. "You never met my father," said Miss Edith, and that closed the subject.

Sam blossomed. Clean overalls every week. Watched where he spit. Miss Edith even let Hogan sleep in the kitchen, though he had to stay outside during the day. "A reasonable woman," Sam bragged.

Came the Dripping Springs pie supper and Sam took Miss Edith.

She didn't bake a pie for the auction, being new to the community and not wanting to push herself forward. But she was polite and friendly and Sam stood in the back of the schoolhouse with a grin so broad you'd swear it met in back.

Pie suppers follow a formula. There is a lot of joshing by the auctioneer. The teacher says a few words of welcome and the quartet sings gospel songs, old favorites like "Along About the Time That She's Sweet Sixteen" and comic numbers like "I Picked a Lemon in the Garden of Love." Then before the pies are auctioned, they hold the contests for Ugliest Man and Prettiest Girl. The crowd puts money on its choices and the most money wins. Somebody keeps the totals on the blackboard.

Ugliest Man is a joke. Usually every man there will have a dime bid on him and the auctioneer, claiming that it is the hardest decision of his life, will take a quarter from his own pocket and settle the thing.

Prettiest Girl can get serious. Young bucks steamed up over a special girl lay their money down with a will and friends back their play. I have personally seen a Prettiest Girl contest run up to $18.

This one at Dripping Springs had two strong candidates and both were backed heavily. It ran up to $5 before you could turn around. Then some little kid raised his hand and put 8 cents on Miss Edith. Her name went on the blackboard.

The crowd went back to bidding on its favorites and Miss Edith's name stayed up there at 8 cents. Sam got red in the face and shifted uncomfortably. He sidled down front and muttered something to the auctioneer, who pretended to swoon.

"Ten dollars on Miss Edith!" he shouted.

That set off a Prettiest Girl contest people will talk about forever. Maybe you've heard about it already? If so, you know that Miss Edith won at $68 and some odd cents. Shouting, "There may be snow on the roof, but there's still fire in the stove!" old Ival Macklin helped Sam put Miss Edith over the top.

It was the talk of the countryside. In no time at all, Sam found he was having visitors every evening. Male visitors. They'd talk and dawdle and Miss Edith would set out the coffee pot and cut a cake.

Less than a month later she married a farmer from Peace Valley. Hogan moved back into the house and Sam took up the trombone again. Miss Edith was his last fling.

Once in a while I close my eyes and watch my private parade. People who brushed my life pass by again, people I never knew well but won't forget.

Cooney Pratt's Aunt Tootsie had a goat named Hannibal instead of a watchdog and was what we called double-jointed. She could tie knots in twine with her toes and once in a while could be coaxed into a demonstration.

The Pratts, like many hill clans, went west most summers to pick fruit, berries and hops. They would take Tootsie along to watch their kids, or vice versa. Not that Tootsie was too dumb or lazy to work, but she would get to looking at a strawberry, thinking about the snow that fell and melted to fill the reservoir that irrigated the field, the little bugs that stirred the soil to feed the roots and how Tamerlane, the Asian conqueror, had fast riders bring him snow from the mountains to make sherbet. Half an hour later Tootsie would still be looking at that strawberry.

Tootsie stopped a train on a trestle once. She had a good personal reason for being there, but it didn't fit into the Denver and Rio Grande Western Railroad's grand scheme of things.

She married a chap named Elmer Zimmerman who wanted nothing from life but to work, sock away some money in Postal Savings and listen with grave courtesy as Tootsie talked of clouds and frogs and apples and how to make cookie cutters from tin cans.

Sam Womack was as fine a fox hunter as the Eleven Points country ever saw and a good man to neighbor to. It was Sam who went visiting when one of our bachelors passed up local talent and took a bride from another state. "Fine woman," Sam reported. "She grabbed a sack of feed by the ears, flang it over her shoulder and walked off with it." We could hardly wait to meet this paragon.

It was Sam who straightened out the new teacher, a young

man who had demonstrated with an apple and a needle that the earth is round.

The walls seemed to bulge outward next morning as Sam strode down the schoolhouse aisle. Sam was big enough, as the saying goes, to hunt bear with a buggy whip. He had been most everywhere the U.S. Army could send a man, Sam told the teacher, and except for some bumpy places like Fayetteville, Ark., and New Guinea, the earth was flat.

"So don't try no more of your trashy city talk on my kids," Sam warned.

Old Man Dockery was the richest man in our village. He owned the store, the feed mill, a lead mine and farms without number. When a piece of land came up for tax sale, Dockery bought it. He was as tight as the bark on a tree. The story was that Dockery's dogs never learned to scratch because he skinned their fleas for the hide and tallow.

The Christmas I was 5, I got a couple of rolls of caps. No cap pistol. Those cost from 15 cents to a dollar at Dockery's store. Still if you have caps, you can make noise.

I was playing on the boardwalk outside the store a day or so after Christmas. I would tear a cap from the roll, place it on the head of one of the nails that held down the planks and hit it with a rock. Caps don't always fire when you do it that way.

Old Man Dockery watched me for a while.

"No pistol?" he asked. "Nope," I said. He went inside the store and I waited expectantly. I had a pretty good idea of what was going to happen. After all, it was almost still Christmas.

Dockery came back with a rusty old hammer, the claws broken off.

"I'm gonna let you use this," he said, "until you've popped all them caps."

Sometimes I wonder why the doctors down in the hills even bothered. People went to them as a last resort and generally credited any cure to their own homespun ministrations.

Doc Thompson once cornered a patient and forced him to admit that the pills Doc gave him had done some good.

"Well," the man said grudgingly, "even a blind pig finds an acorn now and then."

Doc said he was going to have that painted on his office door.

"Couldn't come to scratch, I was feelin' so porely," Jimmy Brotherton told me once, shaking his head dolefully. "So I went to town and doctored for it. Then I hit one more lick on my own and come around right pert."

Jimmy had been treating himself with sulfur and molasses and tea steeped from sheep droppings. One more lick and he come to scratch. But in the meantime, he had foolishly run up a three-dollar doctor's bill.

Doc Thompson treated me after a horse threw me into a fence, cracking some ribs. "No need to rush right in," Doc said sarcastically when I told him it had happened three days before. "You'd be starting school next month anyway."

Doc was given to bursts of sarcasm. A man came to him with an inflamed appendix. His wife had been giving him turpentine and sugar, but he finally decided to seek a second opinion.

Doc yanked the appendix out just before it burst and then told the man, "Turpentine won't help an appendix as far along as this one. What you should have done was get the left hind foot of a possum, hold it right over the sore spot and sleep one night under a persimmon tree. Best when the moon's full."

"You know, Doc," his patient said, "seems to me I heard my grandma say the very same thing."

"Jesus wept!" said Doc.

Clive Young lived in a tent with a pack of dogs and some goats.

"Dogs and hogs knows," Clive said. He would watch to see what they ate when they felt poorly and do likewise, sometimes to treat an ailment but more often in a spirit of scientific inquiry. After a couple of near-fatal episodes, Clive eliminated goats as medical mentors. "Goats ain't human," he said.

Every fall every mother in the hills would check her medicine chest to be sure she was ready for the cold months. My own interest was in dodging any sort of treatment, so my memory is flawed, I'm sure. But I remember some of the standard remedies.

A little packet of sulfur, yellow and evil-smelling. Mix with lard and apply to rashes. Mix with molasses and take internally. A springtime dosage to thin the blood (or thicken it?) was almost mandatory. In winter you got it on general principles.

Turpentine and sugar were for worms. Any kid who looked puny was suspected of harboring worms. A kid who swallowed a few drops of turpentine with a spoonful of sugar would immediately climb trees, leap fences and tackle chores with gusto. It was that or another dose.

Sassafras tea was another spring tonic to tone up the system. In winter you got it with honey for a sore throat.

There were a few staple boughten remedies: Watkins Ointment for man and beast. Peruna or Hadacol for mysterious adult purposes and blackberry brandy for diarrhea.

My grandmother was known as a boss hand with what she called "yarbs." Once she treated me for some minor ailment. She boiled some dried weeds in water, held my nose and poured a cup of the brew down me.

I drew one shuddering breath when she let go of my nose. My intestines shriveled into a hard knot then began to writhe like a nest of snakes. My eyes bulged and blurred. All I could see were great golden spots forming and exploding. I dropped to the floor and lay there panting like a hard-run dog.

I could hear a shrill keening, the scream of a tormented soul. It was coming from me.

My grandfather watched placidly from his rocker by the stove.

"Lydia," he said approvingly to Grandma, "you got a real good scald on that hog."

We had this school teacher, Miz Holt, an old, old woman. She was old when our superintendent, Timberline Mitchell, still had hair on top of his head.

Tall and skinny, she was, with wrinkled skin and deepset dark eyes with purple shadows under them. She wore black dresses of some hard, shiny material that used to be the uniform for old widows.

She kept on teaching, though nobody knew why. We all figured she was rich. She never spent a nickel. Used to buy day-old bread at Hockstrasser's grocery and raised a big garden on a patch of wasteland near the pottery. You'd see her there, like an animated scarecrow, hoeing and weeding at dawn or way late in the evening.

When Miz Holt began teaching it was about the only job a decent woman could hold. She couldn't have clerked in a store. She was too shy and strange. Never looked you in the eye except when she got excited. Then she would grab you by the arms and put her face right up next to yours. Her fingers would dig into your flesh and her voice would get high and choky. It was kind of creepy.

Everybody knew how Miz Holt kept her job. It was J. T. Kimbrough's desire. Kimbrough was president of the bank, a remote and awesome figure. The bank had all the money in the county and J. T. had the say on who got any of it. That's all we knew about economics.

J. T. could be mean. They tell of a family that skinned the bank on a deal. Years later the bank got their farm, a sorry patch of rocks and scrub timber. J. T. had the buildings torn down, fenced it tight and ran hogs on the place.

People said J. T. was as tight as the bark on a tree, but he lived well. He had a big brick house, a cook and yard man and when he threw a party, he hired extra help from Darktown, the black community up by the sawmill. He bought a new Packard every other year, switching to Cadillacs in later years, and businessmen competed for the privilege of buying J. T.'s trade-ins.

J. T. wore gray suits in the cool months and seersucker ones in summer, along with fancy panama hats. Every other week, Ollie Haslett cut his hair. J. T. would walk halfway around the square to Ollie's shop and his coming was noted. People would nod if J. T. did first and murmur to each other after he passed.

No matter how many men were waiting, they would all claim that they wanted to finish a magazine first or were just loafing. J. T. would nod pleasantly and climb into the chair. The other customers would talk among themselves loudly, like boys showing off. If a remark drew a snort of approval from J. T., the memory would be treasured and the tale repeated often.

Those trips to the barbershop were all we ever saw of J. T., but he had a hand in everything going on—city, county or school district. And old Miz Holt always had a job, because J. T. said so.

She wasn't much of a teacher. The school board moved her around until eventually she settled in as study hall teacher.

We kids used to make her life miserable. We'd sneak out, hide behind the curtains of the stage at one end of the room when she called roll, then emerge after she had laboriously written a list of absentees and make her change it.

Boys and girls would get together at the bookshelves. It drove Miz Holt frantic. One day she caught a couple cuddling (quite antiseptically) and shooed the boy back to his seat. Then she clutched the girl's arms and talked and talked and talked, her voice rising until we all could hear. "Sweet lamb," Miz Holt screamed, "don't you know you could lose your senses and get a baby?"

We kids used to speculate that J. T. and Miz Holt had had something going in years gone by, a ludicrous notion to us.

When Miz Holt's son died, it was the first we knew that she had one.

He was paralyzed and, some said, mentally backward. Miz Holt had tended him alone for 30 or 40 years. His room was full of exercising equipment and a bed that could be raised and lowered. He had a radio and a record player and all sorts of toys to pass the time with. And there were shelves of medicine. Must have cost a fortune, all that stuff.

I was taking a morning stroll during a visit down home when this beat-up old pickup slid to a momentary stop at an intersection, then patched out onto the highway and roared up the hill in my direction. The driver was laying a strip of rubber. Halfway to me, he double-clutched, totally unnecessary with a pickup but satisfyingly noisy. As he flashed by, I recognized Burnall.

I met him when I was a senior in high school, enrolled in a teacher-training course and doing a lot of practice teaching at country schools. Burnall had reached the upper grades of one of those schools by a process of attrition. He had worn out several teachers.

Burnall carried a truck gearshift lever around, complete with knob and the little dingus on the side that you lifted to shift into compound. Sometimes in class he would stick the rod into a crack in the floor and practice shifting. His ambition was to be a big-time truck driver. Scholastically, I suspect his goal was to learn to read traffic signs.

Burnall got his first real chance when Charlie Smith sent him off to the wheat harvest in one of his trucks. Burnall bought a leather belt six inches wide, strapped it on and left town with his eyes shining.

Somewhere out west a wheel came off. Burnall figured he'd better tell Charlie, so he hitchhiked home. Trouble was he couldn't remember where he'd left the truck ... Kansas, Oklahoma, Texas? I never heard how they got that sorted out.

Burnall drove a concrete truck for a while when they were building Bull Shoals Dam. If you want to dig down through about 20 feet of concrete, you'll find it buried there today. Burnall backed up too far with a full load.

In a weak moment, a brother-in-law got Burnall a job delivering new cars. He was to work out of St. Louis, hauling six or eight new Mercurys at once.

Burnall's first trip was down into Arkansas. The boss gave him directions and a warning: An underpass near Jonesboro was too low. Go around it.

Burnall forgot. Ran under the thing and ripped the top off two new cars. By that time, he'd learned to use a telephone, so he called back instead of hitchhiking.

"Gracious," said the boss, or words to that effect. "Well, switch your load around and get those ruined cars on the bottom where people can't see them. Then come on back."

Yeah. You are right. Burnall switched the cars, then drove right back under that low bridge, ripping the tops off two more cars.

Burnall was fired. His boss had to fill out a report for the front office, the drivers' union and for Burnall.

In the blank space after "Reason for Dismissal," the boss wrote, "Dangerously inattentive."

6/The educational process

The week before school started was a time of frantic activity, feverish pleasure-seeking and pure misery for kids and parents in our little community.

The last week of vacation was launched officially by Turk's mother. Turk spent the summers junking old cars for his father and sleeping in the back seat of a wrecked LaSalle. It took his mother a week to get him ready for school. She used P&G bar soap and a scrubbing brush and I think she boiled Turk.

He would come out of the first bath dark gray. You could count off the remaining days of vacation by Turk's changing hue. When school opened he would be pink, bleeding in spots, and his hair would be bleached white except where patches had fallen out.

Meanwhile, the rest of us kids were in the grip of the one-last-time syndrome.

One last raid on the pop truck. A long, long hill just west of town forced loaded trucks to gear down to a crawl. Daredevils on bicycles—on both sides of the road to forestall evasive action—could swoop down on the laboring truck, drag cases of pop from the open racks on its sides and zoom down the hill to safety, loot balanced on the handlebars.

It wasn't as easy as it sounds. Bud Hunziker crashed with a

case of Grapette one day and spent an hour stretched over a sawhorse while we picked slivers of glass from his hide with needle-nosed pliers.

One last excursion to the underground spring canyon on South Table Mountain. A man named Jack Brown, who operated riding stables and pony-ride concessions, leased or owned most of the mountain. When his horses became exhausted, Brown would turn them out to graze and recuperate.

The only water on the mountain was from the spring and we kids used to trap the horses in the narrow canyon, leap aboard them as they trotted past us and ride them down the mountain. They would buck and squeal and eventually pitch us off, usually into a pile of rocks or a patch of cactus.

Town kids, Boy Scouts mostly, would hike to the canyon once in a while. One glorious day Red Herbert, Dale Williams and I convinced T. A. Wadley, the world's rottenest kid, that there were Indian paintings on the walls of the underground spring cavern. We floated him and his official Boy Scout carbide lantern through the narrow opening on an old door, telling him to yell when he wanted to be pulled out by the rope tied to his ankle. Then we tied the rope to a bush and left.

Nadine, Dale's soft-hearted sister, went up and pulled Wadley out after a couple of hours. He must have sweated off 15 pounds.

We three told each other that if we stuck together, Wadley would not dare seek revenge. Several days later Wadley beat the three of us bloody.

Though most of us kids secretly looked forward to school, there were exceptions.

One evening our household was roused by the hammering of hooves. It was Palooka Baughman on his father's Appaloosa stallion. Palooka was 7 years old. Upon completion of first grade, he had informed one and all, starting with his

teacher, that he had had a bellyful of education. Now he was heading for the high country.

Palooka hid out in the hills for several days. Someone finally caught him with a jelly sandwich.

On the night before school opened, the Brewsaws, the Williamses and the Holtens would stroll over to our house. We had the best view of the Borklunds' yard.

The Borklunds had seven children, four of them boys. Just before school Poppa Borklund cut the boys' hair and all the kids had baths in a tin tub behind their house. The tub was out of sight of our front porch but only because it was handier that way. The Borklunds lived their lives for all to see. On haircut night the whole family milled around the yard in various stages of dress or none.

Haircut night took a lot out of Poppa Borklund and he prepared for it by tanking up at the Dew Drop Inne. After supper he would place a kitchen chair in the yard where the porch light fell on it. Momma Borklund stood by with iodine to cover his mistakes and a stack of towels for the bathers.

Poppa would take a firm grip on a kid's thatch and start snipping with his scissors. He liked to leave an inch of white, scarred scalp above the ears. Great hunks of hair would fly. Kids would squirm and protest and when they did, Poppa would lift them off the chair by their remaining hair and cuff them, roaring threats.

Meanwhile, Momma would be supervising the bathing. The kids went by age. Since they heated just one tub for seven baths, you had to wonder whether the littlest ones gained or lost by immersion.

On this particular night Poppa was winding up the haircuts with a truly awesome burst of profanity when one of the girls shrieked.

"Poppa, Poppa," she screamed, "Ansel piddled in the bathtub!"

A naked, dripping boy streaked around the corner of the house, dropped to the ground, rolled under the barbed-wire yard fence and vanished in the dark. Eight Borklunds chased him but eventually returned to the lighted yard one by one. Poppa was the last to return and he seated himself in the barbering chair, arms crossed, staring grimly into the dark.

Just before I went to sleep that night I heard Poppa boom, "Ansel, the longer you stay out there, the worse you're gonna get it."

School bullies seem to be a thing of the past, at least the sort who once ruled with fist and boot and a pack of fawning jackals in the hidden corners of the school grounds and the alleys and lots nearby where teachers never trod. I'm sure the talent is still there, but nowadays a potential bully has many barriers between himself and fulfillment—psychologists, sociologists, police department liaison officers. Besides, modular scheduling and elective courses stagger schedules so that it's difficult for a kid to establish a school-wide reputation.

A bully needs a victim and an audience. When Turk and Taw, the schoolyard bullies of my youth, flourished, everybody went to the same classes at the same time and left school at 4 p.m. What Turk left undone at lunchtime, he could finish at recess. The luckless one who eluded Taw in the morning could be ambushed after school.

Turk had a quarter-inch forehead and a vocabulary of six basic verbs and seven expletives, all of four letters. After school and weekends he helped his father junk cars. When he hit you, his fist would be full of ball bearings.

Taw was a curiosity. He was a rich and snobbish bully. He seemed to feel it was his mission to keep the lower orders in line. Once when Bud Hunziker bled on Taw's shirt, Taw went home and changed it. He braided a leather quirt in manual arts class and wore it by a strap around his wrist. He slashed at my dog Gus once, and Gus bit the quirt off at the wrist. Then he nearly bit the arm off at the shoulder.

One December Bunny Molloy and I designed a cardboard Santa and chimney in sixth grade art class. It was such a hit that we were told to make one 10 feet tall to decorate the gymnasium. We were excused from art and music classes daily to work on it. Then Bunny got sick and the teacher told me I could select a couple of helpers from those who wanted to volunteer.

I picked Turk and Taw because when they raised their hands, everybody else lowered theirs.

I set to work in a room next to the art department. Turk and Taw messed around for a while, then began inspecting the contents of a supply closet. Shelves of paper and paste and stuff ran to the closet ceiling. Turk and Taw climbed the shelves and they ripped loose. The noise was terrific and dozens of jars of paste and paint and turpentine broke. The whole building quivered. There were screams, shouts, then ominous silence. Then footsteps growing louder until the door opened and there stood Timberline Mitchell, the superintendent. "Who did this?" he asked.

I looked at Turk. I looked at Taw.

"I did," I said.

Spring's first sounds were the clank and clatter and scrape of tin cans on the sidewalks around school. Kids fastened them to their shoes by stomping dents in them and then pounding the edges snugly around the soles of the shoes with a hammer or a brick.

It was a short-lived celebration. Neither teachers nor parents would let it go on for more than a few days. Besides, it wasn't much fun. Except, of course, that it drove some teachers goofy.

The only kid who ever made a big name for himself in tin-can stomping was Turk. On a dare, he fastened the cans on in the second-floor boys' restroom and tried to walk to class. He skidded on the first step, hit every other step down to the landing, got up and skidded down the other half of the flight. If Turk had a brain, our shop teacher often said, he'd take it out and play with it.

We kids who lived in the country concealed our tin cans in paper sacks or wrapped them in jackets. Otherwise, the bus driver would confiscate them. In those days, adults stuck together more closely than they do now. They knew the enemy and they made common cause.

I doubt that any of the adults in our county knew what inhibitions were. But if they had, they would have been in favor of them.

Mrs. Hockstrosser, who ran a grocery near school, was typical of the grownups I knew. She wanted the lash brought back. I think it was because of the doughnut game.

Some Hockstrosser doughnuts enjoyed long careers. After a week or two on a tray marked "Fresh Baked Today," they would be transferred to the thrift shelf at half price for a long run. Last stop was an open cardboard box labeled

"Kids' Cookie Jar!" You could have two of anything in there for a penny.

One spring we discovered that the doughnuts which had been lying in the bottom of the box for generations bounced like golf balls if spun edgewise off the finger. The game was to get one out of the box and bounce it out of the store—preferably in front of a customer—before Mrs. Hockstrosser could scuttle out from behind the cash register and jerk out a handful of your hair.

The medical department of our elementary school consisted of a box kept in Miz Bell's desk. It contained a roll of tape, several of gauze, a bottle of iodine and a tin of Watkins Ointment.

Miz Bell used it several times a week, mostly to treat athletic injuries. For a school with an athletic budget of maybe $7 a year, we had a lot of casualties.

Not enough to suit Miz Bell, though, who used to grasp her patients by one ear while pouring iodine into an open wound. "Stop sniveling or I'll snatch you bald-headed," she would sympathize. Shug Gunter, a hyperactive kid, acquired a cauliflower ear in the sixth grade which he blamed on Miz Bell's ministrations. Shug's flat nose he acquired while setting the school record for the coal-bin jump. The lump of scar tissue over one eye came from a rock fight and he still walks funny from several years of anchoring a championship line of crack-the-whip. Championships were determined by body count, the number of schoolmates snapped loose from their moorings and senses.

The coal-bin jump was our most spectacular pastime. It involved climbing an iron ladder up the side of an enormous bin, in itself a dangerous undertaking, then leaping far out onto the huge pile of stoker slag—composed of clinkers of unburnable matter raked out of the furnace along with ashes.

A proper angle of descent had the satisfying effect of shredding the jumper's clothing to rags and leaving him filthy and exultant. Too steep a drop and knees would strike the chin, chipping teeth, while the tailbone disintegrated on impact.

Shug tried a bellywhopper. That, as every witness can testify, is no way to jump into a slag heap. Even Shug agreed with that a day or two later when the swelling went down enough for him to make himself understood.

Rock fights and tree climbing were popular, too, and claimed their share of victims. But nothing provided Miz Bell with as much work as the craze for killing ants that swept the school one spring.

The insects, big red rascals, appeared unexpectedly from nests under the school's crumbling sidewalks. At first we kids made an idle game of stepping on them. Something like hopscotch emerged. Then, overnight, a new game developed.

We'd bring hammers to school. Matches were arranged. Starting at a crack from which ants were pouring, contestants would shuffle along on their knees mashing the ants and singing out their scores. Watchers would investigate claims of multiple kills and cheer their favorites.

Contests would cover one, two or three sidewalk squares. Naturally, we devised ways to cheat. The most effective, we learned, was for a backer of one contestant to slide a foot, often bare, forward to cover an ant or a possibly winning cluster of them. The best way to counter this ploy was to miss your target and hit that foot with a lusty, full-arm swing.

My eldest sister has only a rudimentary scrap of nail on her right big toe. That treacherous girl sided with my opponent the day I almost beat Bud Hunziker. She covered what would have been a winning double-kill for me.

I still claim I had every right.

My sister was a darb with scissors and Mother's Day was her day to shine. I did the best I could.

Kids made their mothers' gifts in our school and you had two ways to go: paper silhouettes or hand plaques.

The silhouettes had class. Teacher would rig a lamp at a desk. The kid would sit beneath it and his shadow, the head in profile, would fall on a piece of paper. Then the kid would trace around the shadow. Or maybe a second person did the tracing and the subject took it from there. I forget. I've tried to blot it all from my mind.

Anyway, after a week of art classes and, to my mind, a lot of unnecessary showing off, those little Leonardos would come up with handsome silhouettes of themselves. They would be cut from black construction paper, pasted on cream-colored paper, with their names and the year printed below. All those pussycats could print beautifully, too.

Some of them—my sister, for one—would cut the cream-colored paper into an oval and paste on a paper lace border. Needlessly ostentatious, I felt. Besides, she just did it to show me up.

I never made a silhouette. Teacher always flunked me out of them after a day or two. It was that or blow the whole room's supply of construction paper. I couldn't cut along a line.

"Take a breath between each cut," teacher told me once. "Let it out and cut just a little way along the line, then take another breath."

No use, I'd sweat and groan, bite my tongue, but always lop off my chin or my nose or take a divot from my hair. Teacher would take the scissors away, hand me a lump of wet clay and tell me to make a plaque.

What you did was pound the clay into a flat cake, press your hand firmly into it, scratch your name on it with a nail and, when it dried, paint it. I made plaques from the first through the fifth grades.

Mother's Day projects began two weeks early. They would be finished in a week, displayed in the classroom for a week and taken home the Friday before the big day. Bus drivers loved that day. We would sit stiffly, quietly, preserving our treasures. If the bus hit a bump, we would squall in fright.

In sixth grade I made an ashtray. Still limited to clay, you see. It was such a disaster that Red Herbert organized a naming contest. Patricia Fertig won with "Bad Dog."

In seventh grade I got into shop class. I decided to make Mom a breadboard shaped like a pig. It went well until time came to cut it out with a jigsaw, which, I discovered, is just a different kind of scissors. I lopped off the front foot and the tail.

The shop teacher said it couldn't be salvaged—and Mother's Day the next Sunday. "But maybe I've got something you can use," he said. He dug up a picture frame that a talented student had almost finished the year before. All I had to do was sand and varnish it.

My mother was delighted. She made a fuss over me. Then she used that frame for one of my sister's silhouettes. An understanding woman, my mother, but she did have her blind spots.

We came to high school from places called Peace Valley, Eleven Points, Dripping Springs, Lebo, Hocomo. We would stand at the mail box in winter dark; some of us might walk a mile to the crossroads where we would be picked up by a yellow bus.

At school we would mingle with the town kids, but it was an uncertain, standoffish relationship at best. Mostly we stuck with our own kind.

We'd carry our lunches, eat them in the gym. There was no lunchroom. There would be noontime intramural sports, two 20-minute games of volleyball or basketball. Almost all of the players were country kids.

Our real school life was lived on the bus, an hour or two morning and evening.

In between we ricocheted off the curriculum. English, math, government, "fizz-ed" (calisthenics for kids who got up at 4:30 to milk, feed hogs, split wood) and two electives. Generally teachers did the "electing" for us.

During the bus rides we'd try to sort out these experiences, come to terms with ourselves and make a place for ourselves in the little bubble of society to which we were consigned. We couldn't choose our companions; we made do with what we got.

Each bus had a princess, cool and gracious, unattainable except perhaps for one chosen boy. The rest of us watched these royal romances with breathless interest and delight. We were loyal to our princess. A heckler once derided ours. "Looka them teeth. Eat corn off the cob through a knothole." He was flattened. "Whupped solid and had it coming," said our bus driver. "They got some trashy people down around Hocomo."

The princess had her court; the top boy had his. There would be a bus clown, an intellectual, a loner, a sporting type who would sneak off at noon to the used-magazine store and buy dirty pictures. Only slightly bawdy postcards

actually, but they caused a stir. Our driver would confiscate them. Nothing escaped his eye.

Hubert (Prof) Profitt drove the Dripping Springs bus for 18 years, a portly, solemn man who maintained order with a minimum of fuss. Fights broke out often on many buses, almost never on Prof's. I saw one flurry of fists. Prof stopped the bus immediately. "Out," he said and out the two boys went, to walk six and eight miles home, respectively.

The last day of school was bus picnic day. The division between town and country was never more marked than on that day, but with a difference. Town kids picked up report cards and dispersed for the summer. Country kids spent the day swimming, eating and romancing, then drove back to town for a movie. It would be past midnight before Prof got us all home.

Our bus always went to Noblett Dam, along with a dozen others from various schools in the area. By tradition, we took a choice spot at Noblett, next to the canoe dock.

One year another bus tried to claim our cooking spot, though we had arrived first. I learned then how wars start. In an instant we were ready to charge from our bus, to rend and destroy those interlopers.

"Hush," Prof roared, and when we had subsided, he added, "I'll be back directly."

The other bus driver was young, tall, burly. He stood on the dock. Prof, as mentioned, was short, plump and middle-aged. He approached the other driver and spoke. The stranger answered with a smirk.

Prof bumped the guy with his belly, driving him back a pace. The man began to argue. Prof closed the gap and bumped him again.

He drove that claim-jumping driver, bump by bump, clear to the end of the dock.

With his heels dangling over water, the other driver surrendered. He signaled his kids to pack up and they moved to another spot.

Prof came back to us puffing. "Start the fire," he commanded.

7/A peasant's son

Looking back now, I can see that I only knew my father for one summer. I lived under his roof for 17 years, but I made his acquaintance during my 14th summer, when we worked together on the farm that represented his last, best chance for the sort of life he craved.

Pop died 26 years later on that farm. A heart attack felled him on the slope between house and barn and he died alone but not lonely. Every tree, fencepost and stone on that sorry patch of Ozark land held a memory for him. He had left a footprint on every square foot, drawing comfort from his ownership and self-esteem from the evidence of his stewardship.

Hill people are peasants, incomplete without land, uncomfortable except among their own kind and with a familiar sky above them. You find great numbers of them in every industrial city. Colonies of aliens, listening to their own music in tacky bars, listening to transplanted country preachers, settling their disputes in brutal hill fashion. Uncomfortable even with each other unless there are ties of blood or friendship "back home." But at least they speak a common language.

Pop left the hills as a young man and worked at many things. He helped build telephone lines and drove teams of six and eight mules on highway construction jobs. He became a motorcycle racer and traveled with carnivals for a time, fighting all comers in the boxing tent. He was a marvelously gifted mechanic and he settled into that sort of work when he could get it.

But those were hard times and Pop worked sometimes as a day laborer for a dollar or 75 cents or 50 cents. I can remember days on end when breakfast was a bowl of oatmeal with a little white Karo syrup over it and supper was fried potatoes and condensed-milk gravy. Nothing in between.

I can remember sleeping in the big tin trunk that held most of our possessions on every move. My sister, two years younger, slept in the opened lid. And one of my earliest memories is of what must have been a bonanza week for Pop. He brought home a sack of groceries—corn meal, a slab of bacon and some eggs. My parents left me alone with my sister for a few minutes and, apparently with some idea of preparing a meal, I got a pan and mixed water and cornmeal in it, broke the eggs and dropped the bacon into the mess. When I realized what I had done, I helped my sister onto the bed and hid under it.

Pop never whipped me, not once. But during the summer I'm thinking of now, he told me that he came within an instant of killing me that evening. "I opened the door and saw that mess," he said, "and I leaped for you. The blood was roaring in my head and I had you by the neck and leg when I come to my senses."

He laughed, a little shakily. That's what I remember mostly about the summer I made my father's acquaintance, the laughter.

Pop's laughter often puzzled me during my childhood. Sometimes it frightened me. Not when we were listening to a radio comic. That I understood. But his personal humor baffled me. I understand it now. It was the mocking, self-deprecatory laughter of a working man who always comes up a dollar short, whose plans are always thwarted by the unexpected—a sick kid, a $10 coal bill that should have been $7, a lay-off at the shop or a short week.

Pop left the hills, but the hills had made him and he was an alien in the city. Three times during my childhood he got a stake together and we returned to the Ozarks only to be driven out, starved out literally.

But this time, the summer after I turned 14, he had a chance to make it. Cash for the down payment, enough left to buy dairy cows. Milk prices were high and there was a government subsidy to boot. He had a little time, breathing room, and a son big enough to help.

Pop laughed all that summer. He told me tales of his youth, the happy times. We worked from 4:30 in the morning till dark and I loved every minute of it. Pop was a strong man and I turned lean and hard, exulting in my strength. There was nothing we couldn't do together.

And the gods smiled on us. Great patches of blackberries had grown up in the untended fields of our farm. Berries brought a wondrous price, 50 cents a gallon at the canning factory. We picked them and the money rolled in. Then we cut the briars and piled them in the ditches with rocks on top to stop erosion of our fields.

We plowed and made hay with horses. Tractors were not to be had in wartime and we couldn't afford one anyhow. Pop amazed me with his knowledge. If you plow with three horses, as we did, you need an equalizer on the single-trees to even the pull. Pop took a piece of oak and made one. We used three horses to pull that walking plow because they were sorry, unmatched animals loaned to us by neighbors for their keep. Neighbors who had tractors.

We milked 25 cows morning and night by hand. But we knew that if things kept going well there would be a milking machine some day. And a tractor with a two-bottom plow.

Pop's example and his laughter and the solid satisfaction of work that he opened up to me that summer kept me afloat. Every day, it seemed, I learned something new about him.

We were cutting out a fence row, trees 20 years old. Some were big enough for corner posts, the others we would haul to the house and cut for fuel. I disturbed a nesting quail and she hopped along in front of me, dragging a wing, then took off with the thunderous sound of the bobwhite's beating wings.

"Watch out," Pop warned me. "She'll flog you."

That little bird? I didn't believe it. I said so.

It was, I believe, the first time I'd ever questioned a statement of my father's. The dour, taciturn man I'd grown up with simply made statements and I accepted them. But our relationship had changed and at that moment I realized it.

I pressed him. Had he ever been flogged by a bobwhite? Had he ever seen it happen?

He, too, realized that something new was happening between us.

"No," he said. "That's just a story everybody tells. I doubt if it's true."

I felt different about Pop from that moment on. Better. I had tested him and he had told me the truth.

When fall came, the day to return to school, I didn't want to go. I walked the half-mile to the corner where the bus would stop, then turned around and went home. I asked Pop if I could lay out of school for a year and work with him. He needed the help, I said, and I'd skipped two grades. It wasn't as if I would be taking longer than normal to finish school.

No, Pop said, I'd better get my education while I could. There was no telling what would happen if I didn't.

I was soon caught up in the things that high school students consider important, and Pop and I drifted apart. The memory of that summer faded and I left home for good at 17. But at least I made my father's acquaintance before he died.

My boyhood ambition was to tame lawless towns with my blazing sixguns. I might be in that line of work today if I had mastered a proper squint. All the western heroes I read about or watched in Saturday afternoon movies had these neat squints. They didn't call 'em squints, of course.

Destry, hero of my all-time favorite western novel, would narrow his eyes in moments of stress and they'd give off these steely glints. For gunslingers going up against him that glint was "an early glimpse of perdition," if I recall Max Brand's phrase correctly.

Hopalong Cassidy's eyes narrowed to slits when he was riled. His sidekick, Lucky, would mention that once or twice every movie.

One movie impressed me tremendously. The hero was a shabbily dressed drifter who rode into this town looking for his brother only to learn that he had been shot to death under mysterious circumstances while helping some small ranchers in their troubles with a cattle baron who was fencing off the water holes. Great plot; I don't know how they come up with them.

Anyway this drifter took a lot of abuse in the first two reels and people generally figured him for a loser, but this oldtimer said that he had ridden with Kit Carson and Wild

Bill Hickok and this drifter had the same look about him. "Looky them eyes," the oldtimer said, "that's the look of the eagle." Sure enough the drifter was masquerading. Turned out to be the fastest gun west of the Pecos and, if you missed the film, the cattle baron was in league with the land agent who knew a railroad was coming through the valley and when the drifter "put the quiiiieeetus" (the oldtimer's description) on the villains, the small ranchers stood to make a nice piece of change.

Anyhow, I set about acquiring "the look of the eagle."

I practiced in my room, in the chicken house and in the bathroom where there was a mirror. Had to stop that when my mother threatened to dose me with Epsom salts. I'd throw my head back and narrow my eyes until the tears turned me blind. Got it down pat finally, good enough to spring on my schoolmates.

It didn't impress them. Pat Fertig didn't even notice the look of the eagle. She said if I didn't lower my chin, the next rain shower would fill my nose and drown me. Red Herbert saw the narrowed eyes but didn't pick up on the steely glint. I reminded him of his brother when he came down with pink-eye. Red said it so often that next day several mothers sent notes saying to keep their kids away from me. I had to go to the school nurse.

Miz Bell took a close look, cuffed me on the ear and told me to stop squinting.

I couldn't!

I had practiced the look of the eagle so long that it had become habitual. I could hold my eyes wide open, but as soon as I relaxed or my mind wandered the old squint came back. Miz Bell said to hell with it, cuffed me again, took me back to class and told the teacher I was simply crazy as a feed store 'coon.

Naturally my mother did not accept Miz Bell's diagnosis. And I wasn't about to enlighten anybody. So my parents decided that I must have strained my eyes with excessive reading and western movies. They forbade any reading not connected with schoolwork.

In a day or two I lost the look of the eagle. But my folks feared a relapse. They kept me off books, or tried to, for the entire summer vacation. I nearly went mad.

That summer I memorized the labels of Pet milk, Karo syrup, Del Monte ketchup and every other staple in our kitchen. Up to a few years ago I could still recite most of them. The town librarian had been warned to shut me off, but my folks forgot the Christian Science reading room. I would slip in, grab the latest pamphlets and hide in the men's restroom for hours.

I turned to crime. There was a Montgomery Ward catalog in the Borklunds' outhouse. I swiped it. I stole magazines from the Foss and Alpine drugstores. I'd hide at night in our cellar and read them by candlelight. Nearly set myself on fire once or twice. I would sneak a Bible, printed in the world's tiniest type, out of my mother's dresser and read it under my bedsheet. I'd put my bedside lamp under the sheet, too, so my folks wouldn't notice. Do you have any idea how much heat a lightbulb can generate under a sheet on a hot summer night?

It's a wonder I didn't ruin my eyes for real that summer. But it was several decades later that I began to notice that my fingertips were blurred when I cleaned my nails. Have to get reading glasses one of these days, I'd think. Then I was holding books at arm's length. Eventually I began to read sideways, holding the book in the fingertips of one hand. You can stretch farther that way. I found myself backing up against a wall of the bedroom to comb my hair. The mirror is on the opposite wall.

Then my eyes gave final notice. One day I barely managed to complete a piece I was writing. The next morning I could not read a newspaper. Nature's way of getting your attention, I was told. Reading glasses will solve the problem.

So after all these years, my mother's fears came to pass. But I noticed something one morning as I leaned against my bedroom wall trying to get my part straight. My head was thrown back. My eyes were narrow slits. The glint in them could only be described as steely.

The look of the eagle!

Anybody know where I could pick up a set of ivory-handled sixguns?

Poverty is greatly overrated by some of the people you see bopping around town in patched jeans. It is palatable only when you have money. Or to put it another way, poverty is a virtue only when it is not a necessity.

The spring the bat factory in my hometown laid off half its work force—me—and my roomie Dinger pulled a hamstring muscle, our lives got down to a matter of basic survival. For two or three months we had to do the best we could. We learned that this is a greatly overcrowded field.

I was assistant foreman at the bat factory. The other employee was plant superintendent. Orlo, his name was. I used to point out that there was a gap in the table of organization and ask whether I couldn't be foreman. "In time, boy," Orlo would say. "In time."

Orlo was really into baseball bats. We made them for the St. Louis Browns—not the big club, their farm teams. As far as I was concerned, one billet of second-growth ash was just like the other 20,000 I shifted from rack to kiln to lathe to packing box every day. But Orlo claimed that a man could spend his life making baseball bats and learn something new every day.

"Tricks to the trade, boy," he would say. "Tricks." One trick was for the plant superintendent to goof off in the office reading Rangeland Romances while the assistant foreman moved mountains of ash billets through their life-cycle.

Orlo kept a Louisville Slugger in the office. He would heft it every so often and spit contemptuously. "A trademark and varnish," he would say. "That's all they got, boy." He dreamed of the day when Ted Williams or Stan Musial would somehow lay hands on one of his creations and discover that the Stradivarius of bat-makers lived in the Ozarks.

When we had enough bats in stock to supply the Browns' organization for half a century or so, it was decided to close the factory except for a one-man maintenance crew. Orlo broke the news at 11:15 one morning. Since it was short notice, he paid me clear up till noon.

If you are not familiar with the way news gets around a small town, let me tell you that it is swifter than laser. I walked into my rooming house at 11:30 and my landlady had her hand out. She had a new policy: one week's rent in advance. I went to the cafe where I had been putting an occasional meal on the tab and instead of my bowl of chili, the owner brought my outstanding account. He had a new policy too. Then Dinger came up lame.

Dinger grew up in Colorado and moved to the farm adjoining ours when his mother married the owner. His real name was Roy, but he found that Ozark males either had two names—Joe Bob, Johnny Jack, or the like—or nicknames like "Dobber" and "Pud" and "Bubba." He thought that was the funniest thing he'd ever run across, so he made up the goofiest nickname he could think of for himself. Everybody accepted it. He is a college professor now, a man of considerable clout on a university campus. But every so often some acquaintance spots him and hollers "Dinger!" across a crowded room.

At that time Dinger was a third baseman by trade. He could purely hammer a baseball. That didn't pay anything, not on our town team, but a local florist paid Dinger $25 a week to drive his delivery truck when necessary and to stroll over to the florist's box at games and chat with him and his friends.

Flowers were not a major industry in our town. There would be a run on sweetpea corsages for the junior-senior prom and flurries at Mother's Day and Easter. No florist needed a deliveryman too lame to play ball, so Dinger was given his outright release.

After a few days I got work with the local radio station. I was the entire news staff, the "Voice of Sports" and also a standby disc jockey for Ramblin' Rhythm, our nightly record show. My day began at 7 a.m. and by midnight, when we signed off the air, I had worked up a heck of an appetite. My salary was $25 a week. Our room rent was $7.

Dinger made a fair thing out of shooting pool for a couple of weeks. Then an old dink in a denim jumper asked him to teach him the game. Dinger was holding all our money (I couldn't be trusted, he said, to walk past a hamburger joint) and in a hour's time, that old geezer had it all.

Once a week, we would borrow a car, put 50 cents worth of gas in it and drive to our folks' farms. We would present each of our mothers with one-half of our accumulated laundry and eat everything they had in the house. Dinger ate 14 pancakes at our place one night. My mother was amazed. If we hadn't stopped at his folks' first, he really would have showed her something. Dinger's stepfather said he hadn't seen anything like our visits since the grasshopper plagues drove him out of Oklahoma.

The local hotel featured Sunday brunch, all you could eat for $1.50. We went once. The manager stopped us as we left. "Never again, gentlemen," he said. "Not ever."

Our landlady put a padlock on her refrigerator.

Dinger went on a wiener roast with a girlfriend's family. After a few minutes, they all sat back in awe. The girl's little sister reached for the last cookie on the platter and caught sight of Dinger's face. She shrieked and burst into tears. They claimed the kid had nightmares for a week.

Romance was out of the question for us, but one day I succumbed and invited a lass named Annalee to meet me for a Coke. Dinger was holding our last dollar bill. He handed it over when I promised to return 90 cents change.

"I think I'll have a cherry soda," Annalee told the waitress. "And a grilled cheese sandwich."

That evening I went to see a man I knew slightly, a building contractor. I told him the tale. He laughed until he choked. He gave Dinger and me jobs in another town. He advanced us $50 each. When I left, he was wheezing with laughter again.

I never saw Annalee again. Somebody told me that she married and got real fat. I don't doubt it.

Some kid left a slingshot in our backyard recently and I swiped it. Dumb kid. Nothing for which he abandoned that slingshot could be half as much fun.

He'll want it back, I know, but tough luck, buddy. I gave it to a woman at the office. She was enchanted. Duke it out with her, kid, and best of luck.

I relinquished the slingshot because I felt the stirrings of a familiar impulse, one I know well to be irresistible. Even now I can see it at work on that woman.

She has been dinking around with the slingshot, showing it to visitors. But I passed her office door a while ago and she was holding it, one hand gripping the handle of the peeled elm fork, thumb and second finger of the other hand clasping the pouch while her forefinger guarded the pocket. An atavistic impulse was guiding her.

She is in the power of a force stronger than human will. Pretty soon she will have to use that slingshot. She won't be able to stop herself.

I am curious as to what ammunition she will select. Something soft, I expect.

For indoor work, the kids I grew up with favored clay. Dig a lump from the creek bank and stick it in your pocket. Pinch off a small amount and roll it between your palms until you have a pellet of the proper size and consistency. It makes a lovely thwack when it strikes and it will stick to hair or any rough fabric.

T. A. Wadley, a rich kid, had outstanding success with gumdrops. I suppose they are still available, though I haven't seen any for years. Perhaps M and M's, which don't melt in the hand, would be practical. There would be no evidence.

Probably, though, she will be caught early on. That first successful shot is so gloriously satisfying that you tend to pause, to marvel, to gloat when you should be covering your tracks.

Miz Bell, our school nurse, caught me although I had done everything right. I was wearing a loose shirt, slingshot tucked in my waistband under cover. I waited for the right moment. The blob of clay hit Red Herbert on the right ear, filling the hole.

Absolutely beautiful. But instead of whipping the slingshot back to its hiding place, I sat rejoicing with it in my hand under the desk top. Miz Bell, passing the room, saw its reflection on a window pane. She confiscated it. Then she rapped me twice on the head with her knuckles. My eyes spun around like two marbles in a sink. They almost changed places, I do believe.

Later, in health class, I asked for the slingshot back. "You will never lack for gall," Miz Bell said. "If I wasn't a lady I would kick your butt up between your eyebrows." But she was so astounded by the request that she forgot to slug me again.

When I picked up that slingshot in the yard the other day, I was reminded once again that my father must have been one of the most patient men ever to live.

Memories of the first slingshot I made came back. We stored junk in an unoccupied room of our house. I entered it, cut a chunk from an innertube and the tongue from one of Pop's workshoes. If I thought at all, which is doubtful, I must have assumed that they had been discarded. They hadn't.

Pop became aware of my project when he saw me climbing an apple tree with a saw. The pieces from the innertube and his shoe were on the ground. He surveyed the evidence and drew the right conclusion, but he said nothing. He directed me to another tree and suggested a good forked limb. He explained that the bark should be peeled. Otherwise it would be slippery and soon would begin to decay. He showed me how to wrap string to secure the rubber strips to each branch of the fork and how to attach them to the pouch. There is a trick to that. If you cut a simple slit in the leather it will soon tear.

Then Pop showed me how to use it. Left arm always steady, a firm base. Right arm providing all of power to stretch the

rubber strips. "Look at your target," Pop said. "With practice, your eye and arm will make the right adjustment (for
wind, distance and movement) automatically."

Best of all, Pop didn't warn me not to shoot at livestock or
poultry. He knew I would anyway. And he didn't tell me for
several days that the innertube and shoes had been new.

I became quite expert. If old slingshotters ever organize, I'd
like to join and swap stories. My all-time greatest shot
involved the aforementioned T. A. Wadley, a fat bully.

Cooney Pratt's Aunt Tootsie gave me three bantam chicken
eggs one day. She knew my mother was about to set a hen.
"Put these under the mother," Tootsie said, "and you will
soon have three lovely little friends."

Probably I'd be a finer person today if I had followed her
advice. But I took the eggs to school.

Wadley was scratching a ring for marbles, his backside an
inviting target. Without conscious thought I whipped out
my slingshot, fitted an egg in the pouch and let fly. The egg
hit dead center. It left a delightful sticky yellow splotch.

Wadley bloodied my nose and split my lip. Miz Bell put
iodine on the wounds. I laughed through both experiences.

My father wrote me one letter in all of his life. I was in
college and had written home for $25 to finance some
project or other.

Pop's reply was written with an indelible pencil on ruled
tablet paper. If you remember, you had to lick an indelible
pencil to make it work. After a juicy larrup, it would make
bold purple marks. As it dried, the marks would become

thinner and lighter, finally turning into scratches. Lick again.

Every family had an indelible pencil. It was reserved for important business. When you sold a cow or hog or wrote a check or filled out the monthly postcard showing how much electricity you had used, you got out the indelible pencil.

I can recite my father's letter: "Dear son, Your mother says to watch the spending. Ha. Daisy is milking better this time." That's all there was. No closing. He signed his full name, as if it were a legal document.

The envelope contained $10. Daisy was my Jersey heifer. She'd just had her second calf. Now let me tell you about a note my father wrote once.

It was the only written message my mother ever received from Pop, she said. She didn't count a postcard from Florida showing a fat lady in a tight dress and some hayseed leering at her.

Now this note was written in Oak Creek, Colo. In those years our family periodically was starved out of the Ozarks. Pop would then move us to Colorado and work in a garage to get together a bankroll to get us back to the Ozarks so we could starve some more.

Pop worked 60 hours a week for $20 at Oak Creek. I was about 2 years old. My oldest sister was fixing to get born. My mother's sister, Belle, came to Oak Creek to help mother. My mother's name was Myrtle. Aunt Belle didn't like Pop. All of this matters.

One evening when Belle was a bit crankier than usual, Pop seized the chance to walk downtown and buy some meat for the next day. On the way he had to pass the garage where he worked.

A customer was there alone. The night mechanic had gone off somewhere with the tow truck. The customer was driving a truck, but his problem was with a car stalled somewhere up a mountain road. Pop agreed to ride out to the car and try to start it. If he couldn't, they would tow it back with the truck.

Pop started the car and decided to drive it back to town to make permanent repairs. The customer was to follow in the truck, but for some reason he delayed a few minutes and was far behind Pop when what happened happened.

A bolt holding the car's steering system together snapped just as Pop drove across a bridge. The car made a right-angle turn and sliced through the wooden railing. It landed in a deep hole and sank to the bottom.

It happened so suddenly that Pop needed a few seconds to sort things out. He was sitting in an air bubble and wasn't frightened. He opened one window a crack and let the car fill with water. That equalized the water pressure and he was able to open a door. He swam ashore.

The current was swift and Pop was deposited far downstream from the bridge. It was easier to walk back to town along the creek bank than to climb back up to the road in the dark. It was farther along the creek, but easier.

Pop walked it, cold and wet and awfully tired by the time he got there. He went first to the garage, where he had some dry coveralls. Still no night mechanic there. He went on home. Nobody around.

Everybody was up at the bridge. The customer in the truck had seen the broken railing and had highballed it into town to give the alarm. Everybody turned out, one neighbor thoughtfully stopping to pick up my mother, Aunt Belle and me.

My mother was crying. Aunt Belle was holding me and controlling her grief rather well. She later admitted that her thoughts had turned toward the future and a well-to-do widower who'd always had a yen for mother. Everybody else was having a fine time.

They found Pop's jacket downstream and after a while, it was agreed that his body was bound to wash up on a sandbar down by town. They went to look there. Mother and Aunt Belle went home.

Pop's wet shoes were the first thing they saw. Then through an open door they saw Pop sound asleep in bed. On the kitchen table was a note.

"Myrt," it said. "I forgot the meat."

You could take a regular train from Little Rock to St. Louis in those days and then ride this little puddle-jumper across southern Illinois to Peoria. The cars were old, dirty, smelly and not a place you'd choose to be on a winter evening with $7 in your pocket.

Little Rock hadn't been much fun, either. As a small-town publisher I knew had said, there had been a reporting job waiting for me. He had set it up. He hadn't told me, though, that the newspaper employees were on strike. The job was as a scab.

I had talked with the pickets, reclaimed my cardboard suitcase from the YMCA and bought a ticket to Peoria. A friend there had been urging me to come up, saying he would stake me till I found work. I had his address and phone number and, as mentioned, $7 left.

The puddle-jumper reached Peoria about 10 p.m. There was slush on the streets and snow falling, dirty before it hit the pavement. I called. No answer. Later I learned that the landlady was as deaf as a fence post. I kept calling and walking the streets.

After an hour or so, my blood congealing from cold, I paid

two bits for a ticket at an all-night movie. Now, I've been in tobacco sheds and on fishing boats. I've cleaned septic tanks and worked two days in the offal room of a packinghouse. But that movie was the ripest enclosure I've ever entered.

It was packed. I was about the only patron who hadn't brought a bottle of wine in a paper sack. And maybe the only one who had had a bath during that calendar year. I stuck it out for an hour and began walking the streets again. Too late to be phoning.

Somehow the night wore away. There was a warm lobby by a bus stop, but a cop shooed you out every 20 minutes. When I passed the movie I would pick a popcorn box from the trashbasket out front and line my shoes, which were leaking. At 8 o'clock I took a bus to my friend's boardinghouse.

He had left for California several days earlier, the landlady said. Riding out, I'd told myself that after the night I'd just passed, anything had to be an improvement. A miscalculation.

For $5 a week, the lady rented me a room. More accurately, she rented me half of one of three beds in a room. It had a 25-watt bulb and she gave me a towel I could have read a newspaper through, with more light. No visitors, noise, drinking or eating. Clean towel and sheets every Friday.

A woman at the employment office confided that it was a poor time of year to come to Peoria, but she sent me to a packinghouse. The Man said I didn't look like the type who would stick but he would take a chance. Two weeks till payday, but after one I could draw half a week's pay in advance. Just once. I thanked him. My momma would have been proud of me.

Downtown again, with 80 cents left, I tried a bowling alley. I lied and told the manager I was a boss at setting pins. He let me "double," set two lanes. After 10 minutes he came back, asked wearily, "Why don't anybody ever tell me the truth?" and reduced me to one lane. At 10 cents a game I could make about 40 cents an hour. And all the flying pins I could eat.

That first night I worked till 2 a.m., went to a cafeteria and ate up all but a dollar. Got up at 4:30, rode the bus to work, ate a bowl of chili and macaroni for lunch (30 cents) and returned to the bowling alley after work. Kept that up until I could draw the advance.

My job at the packinghouse was assistant to the time-and-motion engineer, the efficiency expert. I'd stand in one department for hours charting movements and times on one operation, say trimming hams. I was the second most despised person in the plant, next to my boss, who seldom left his office. My presence meant that the company would be trying to raise quotas or cut the crew. Ladies who work in packinghouses acquire a rich and pungent vocabulary. They used it all on me.

Midway in my third week my luck improved. I caught walking pneumonia. I lost 30 pounds, my head was hot and I got to where I couldn't see my charts for all the spots dancing in front of my eyes. The Man said he'd known all along that I wouldn't stick. He paid me off.

My brain was smoking with fever and all I could think of was following my friend to California. But I didn't have enough money. I looked down the list of cities and fares at the bus depot and spotted Lincoln, Neb. That's where I had attended college, worked several places including a newspaper, knew people. And I had the fare.

I bought a ticket and arranged to be routed through the town where a young lady I'd become engaged to was working and, I hoped, waiting. I'd told her that I could make a good living in journalism, which is what sent me off to Little Rock in the first place. I wanted to tell her that everything was going just fine.

She must have believed me because we were married the next spring. But first I had to get to Nebraska. Somewhere around St. Joe the fever burned out and I arrived lightheaded, shaky but okay.

The people I'd known in Lincoln, students mostly, had

moved on. But there was Walt Dobbins, sports editor of the Journal. I caught him as he was leaving the office. No, Walt said, no openings. But what had I been up to? To my amazement I heard myself telling him everything.

He'd check around, Walt said, and I should look him up that evening at the Elks Club. Walt generally closed the bar there. I was there at 6, at 7 and at 8. Walt wasn't. I had 37 cents and Lincoln didn't even have an all-night movie. At 9 o'clock I asked the steward if I could leave a message. The bartender heard me and said Walt had left an envelope for me that afternoon.

In it were two $20 bills and a note: "Got you a job starting Monday."

8/Bulls and
other buddies

At one time my father had a pretty good dairy herd, thanks to the untiring efforts of a magnificent herd bull named Rosebud.

With the fiscal prescience that runs in our family, Pop built up his herd just in time for the collapse of the milk market and the lowering of government subsidies right after World War II. But that doesn't detract from Rosebud's achievements.

Rosebud had a bad name in the Eleven Points country. A real mean bull, people said. He wasn't actually, just misunderstood.

He had a strong sense of territorial rights and he resented intruders. That's why he put so many quail and squirrel hunters up trees. And he was persistent. He'd keep them there until Pop or I came and got him.

Rosebud's record, I believe, was four hours. He had two hunters perched in saplings that time. He'd shake one sapling for a while then move over to the other. They were limber, whippy trees and those hunters could have spent a hundred dollars on the rides at an amusement park without getting half the thrills.

Pop pointed that out, but the hunters weren't a bit grateful. There's no pleasing some people, Pop said, after I had

snapped a chain onto Rosebud's nose ring and we were leading him away.

One of the hunters had held on to his shotgun for a little while and he had peppered Rosebud once or twice before he had to drop the gun and use both arms to hang on to the tree. For the record, you can't convince a grouchy bull of anything with birdshot.

That other incident over at the schoolhouse was a total misunderstanding, as will be made clear.

Rosebud loved to be brushed. He would stand forever, eyes closed and groaning in ecstasy, while you went over him with a curry comb or an old broom.

Scrubby little cedar trees grew here and there on our farm and Rosebud would search them out and rub against them, lean on them until he had flattened them. Then he would roll on them. Quite a sight, a 1,600-pound bull rolling and bellowing. The mail carrier ran off the road one day when he saw Rosebud at it. He thought Rosebud had somebody down and was mauling him.

The schoolhouse was on one corner of our farm about a quarter of a mile back in the woods.

Rosebud spotted the schoolteacher from the woods one spring day. She was sweeping the steps. Rosebud stepped over a low spot in the fence and ambled over, hoping to mooch a brushing. The teacher was unaware of his presence until he nudged her with his cold wet nose.

Things got a little hectic. The teacher squawked in terror and galloped off in all four directions. The kids swarmed like hornets and started throwing rocks at Rosebud. That riled him. He chased them all inside. The kids and teacher clustered near the door, peeking out. Rosebud, circling the building, found an open window, stuck his head inside and bellowed loud enough to loosen shingles. Every kid in the schoolhouse wet his pants.

Pop, who was checking his fences, found Rosebud still circling the schoolhouse. He didn't even try to explain.

One summer Pop and a neighbor, Lee Davis, shared Rosebud's services. Lee had lost his herd bull and Rosebud was more than willing. We'd haul him over to Lee's place whenever one of the ladies in the herd there became romantically inclined and Rosebud would stay until he was needed back home. Then Lee would truck him to us.

One morning an errand took me to the Davis farm. Lee's son, Martin, and I went off to do whatever it was I'd come for. When we returned, Rosebud had climbed onto a platform beside the milkhouse and from it to the bed of the truck I'd driven. He was standing there, leering expectantly.

There is no way to explain such a misunderstanding to a bull.

When Martin and I chased Rosebud off the truck, he went berserk. He bashed in one side of the truck. He uprooted and splintered the loading platform and scattered a dozen 10-gallon milk cans all over the barnyard. Then he started butting a grain drill left nearby. When Martin tried to divert him, Rosebud chased him into the milking parlor. Martin sprinted out the other end, but Rosebud stayed inside long enough to rip down two rows of stanchions. Then he withdrew to the shade of a chestnut tree where he pawed and bellowed for a while and finally lay down to sulk.

118

Lee Davis had been in the house. He came out and surveyed the damage quietly.

"Well," said Lee, "I can't really blame him."

It used to be that you'd see a dog in almost every pickup truck parked on the square or around the two livestock auction barns. People brought them along to work or for company or to show off or swap. It is hard to explain how large a part dogs played in our lives.

They worked with us. They guarded our homes and livestock. The only truly happy times of some men were in the woods or fields with their hunting dogs.

Foxhounds were the aristocrats—strong, tireless, fierce beasts, most of them. Hounds look friendly, sort of cuddly. Don't believe it. Ozark foxhunting is done at night on a hilltop, sitting around a fire and listening to the dogs cast for a fox's spoor and drive it to cover. It can take all night and cover miles. The dogs' voices are distinctive and hunters, who know the hills, fields, creeks and woods like their own kitchens, listen intently, piece the action together and argue amiably and softly about whose dog is doing what. It is bad manners to show excessive emotion.

Foxes are not killed. The same ones are hunted for years. Hunters, dogs, foxes grow to know each other well. When a fox reaches its den, the hunt is over. The dogs are recalled by voice or horn.

Coonhounds, bird dogs, beagles and feists (little mongrels used to hunt squirrels) ranked below foxhounds in the Ozark caste system. A gun-shy bird dog shamed its owner. Woody Smith traded such a dog to a neighbor once and declined to take it back. The neighbor renamed the dog

"Woody" and took it everywhere. He would snap his fingers or bang the truck door to start the dog quaking in terror, then tell watchers its name and where he got it. Woody took back his dog.

Our Queenie was a premier cow dog. My father guaranteed her pups—"natural heelers"—and every one of every litter was snapped up at weaning age. Queenie's amours were closely watched. A neighbor who saw an unsuitable male snooping around our place would chase him off.

Sic an ordinary dog on a cow and it will go for the cow's nose. Queenie's type nips the heels, which is as it must be if a dog is to herd cattle. She would bring in the dairy cows by herself morning and evening, leaving dry cows, heifers and steers. When we turned a cow dry, it took Queenie only a day to realize it. She'd leave that one with the others until it calved.

I can't remember the name of the girl I had my first formal date with, but I remember the look on my dog's face when I told him he couldn't go. I nearly gave up women right there. Old Ricky went everywhere with me and had done so for years. When I began driving he'd get in the truck cab or hop on the back or drape himself on a fender to watch for rabbits. He didn't like it in town and never rode all the way. He'd hop off two or three miles from home and trot back, visiting neighbors on the way. People like the Lee Smiths, who liked fried chicken but not white meat. Mrs. Smith would save the breasts for me or Ricky, whichever got there first.

Ricky was a watchdog and a good one when strangers came around. Trouble was that Ricky knew more people than we did. That made it easy for Luther, a young buck who lived a couple miles up the road.

Dad kept a barrel of gasoline behind the house. When Luther ran short, he would take a couple of gallons. Late at night. Without asking. Ricky would greet him as he climbed the orchard fence, escort him to the barrel then back to the fence and wag good-by as Luther walked back to his Chevy.

My folks spotted Luther several times but never made a fuss. He became so bold he used the orchard gate instead of sneaking up.

Luther's final raid came on a spring night when we'd turned the cows into the orchard to crop the new grass. About 11 o'clock I was lying half awake looking at a full moon outside my window when I heard Luther's old pickup chug up the hill to the corner of our farm about half a mile away, then stop. Pretty soon (or "directly," as they say down home) I heard Luther's shoes crunching on the gravel by the gate. I sat up on the edge of the bed and saw Ricky greet him. Then the two of them went out of sight around the house.

A few minutes later Luther came into view again, carrying a can. As he reached the gate, a window of my parents' bedroom slid up and my mother's voice shrilled:

"Luther, shut that gate! We got the cows up in the orchard!"

———————————————

Gus had reared up with his paws planted wide apart on the back of our living room armchair and was snuffling at the back cushion. I wondered what he was up to. Then, as I came a step or two nearer, I saw that my mother was sitting in the chair, white-faced, paralyzed, tears coursing down her cheeks.

My mother was a little Irish dumpling who feared neither man nor beast nor the powers of darkness, but Gus was something else. He was a pointer who forgot to stop growing until he stood six inches taller at the shoulder than any bird dog I've ever seen. He had a disposition that defies description. (Cooney Pratt's Aunt Tootsie, who believed in reincarnation, theorized that Gus once rode with Attila the Hun.) Gus loved and obeyed two people, Tommy Davidson, the man who raised him, and me.

That confrontation in the armchair was my mother's first meeting with Gus. I'd thought my folks were at a neighbor's house, and I'd let Gus in our back door while I went to tell my parents that Tommy had given me a dog. Naturally I hustled home when my father told me Mom was home. Too late, Mom had been sitting by the radio, listening to the radio and eating cherry chocolates when Gus hove into view.

Gus loved candy, so he reared up and helped himself. With shaking fingers my mother fed him the rest of the box, but dropped one chocolate behind her. That was what Gus was rooting for when I arrived.

I performed the introductions and tried to tell her that Gus was just making friends, a blatant lie. You wouldn't believe what that nice lady said to me. I was 25 years old before I learned what one of the words meant.

Over my mother's objections, my father decreed that Gus could stay. "A boy should have a dog," he declared, and my father's word was his bond. Never had it been tested so severely or so swiftly. As he produced that cliche, he patted Gus's head. It took at least five minutes to stop the flow of blood.

Within a week I was a big man in our neighborhood. I automatically batted first in the afternoon game of workup and kids who thought I might bear them a grudge crossed the street when they saw me coming. Gus established himself by killing Elmer Johansen's dog . . . slaughtering seven of the Brewsaws' chickens who wandered into our backyard . . . chasing the Holtens' cat up on top of a garage where it stayed three days . . . dragging a kid off his bicycle when he rode across a corner of our lawn . . . chasing Mr. Weiner, the Happy Home bakery driver, up on top of his truck every morning for a week . . . seizing the mailman by the wrist as he reached from his car to our box.

Our bread was being left at a gas station and our mail two houses down (neither the Brewsaws on one side nor the Johansens on the other would permit us the use of their boxes) but to my mind it was well worth it.

However, the opening of school neared and my mother began to lie awake nights thinking of life alone with Gus while I was in class. My father eagerly seized the opening and found a truck gardener who was looking for a watchdog. Word got around and the day the guy came to take Gus away, most of the neighborhood lined up across the road and cheered. I stood there sniffling.

As soon as the truck disappeared Wilmer Brewsaw and Elmer Johansen ran over and beat hell out of me.

The main part of our barn had double-notched rafters, which indicates that it was built around 1850. I covered those rafter joints with hay, forking it back and tramping it down, frantically trying to keep up with my father, who was pitching it up from the wagonway. When that central part of the barn was full, there was hay enough for a normal winter.

My father knew this. I was driven by his urgency. It was mow and rake with a wary eye on the sky. A red sunrise likely meant rain, trouble if you were caught with hay on the ground. A full moon was good; you could haul an extra load or two after milking. The blacksmith, a ribby old man with pasty skin and knobby joints, worked all night in haying time. You took mower blades for sharpening after dark.

When the rake handle snapped in two, we lost a day having it welded. It rained that night and we lost most of the hay from the big meadow. "We'll be buying hay this winter," was all that my father said. And late that winter we hauled stringy prairie hay from town.

Milk production dropped from nine cans a day to seven and I understood then what my angry sideways yank on the rake handle had meant. But Pop never mentioned it.

Our barn was larger than the old ones on most of the hill farms. It was built when a quarter-section with 40 acres of bottomland and 60 of pasture provided a handsome living for a large family.

Now and then when Pop changed things around, he would find some cut-iron nails, also from around the 1850s. He saved those in a separate can. He found moldering bits of harness, too, and would name them and tell me their purpose before putting them aside to look at on rainy days.

One stall was lined with heavy planking. "Must have kept a stallion here," Pop said, and he found marks where hooves had scored the planks deeply. Sure enough, an old, old neighbor said he remembered "a famous stud that throwed true ever' time." That stallion's services cost a princely $20. Dan, our grumpy old gelding, occupied the regal chamber occasionally, but he didn't give it any tone at all.

It was never lonely in our barn. There were always kittens, for one thing, and kittens go nicely with any weather, mood or task. For several years an enormous blacksnake lived there, calmly going about its business, which was mice, under my father's protection. Even my dog, which slaughtered snakes by the score, understood that.

In late winter and early spring there would be calves, appealing critters, fed from buckets twice a day. If you get the chance, teach a calf to drink. You wet your fingers in the milk and put them in the calf's mouth. As it sucks, lower your hand into the milk. A delightful experience.

Our cows calved in the woods mostly, and finding them could be a chore. When you did, you carried the calf to the barn on your shoulders, the mother bawling and butting along behind you. Those few hours in the woods were all the home life our calves ever had. Milk was our cash crop then, and calves were quickly put on other feed.

Dairy cows don't like having strangers around at milking

time. They are set in their ways and the social ramble has no appeal whatever. But we had a neighbor, a garrulous old coot, who visited only then, when he had a captive audience.

He would stand at the milking parlor door, gabbing away, while the cows stomped and fussed. Cows entering the parlor would balk when they sighted him and refuse to enter their stanchions, so each time we let a batch in, he would duck around a corner out of sight. When he heard the stanchions lock shut, he would reappear and resume his monologue.

One evening he didn't reappear. We paid no attention, grateful for small blessings. That batch of cows was the last, as it happened, and Pop and I began carrying the 10-gallon cans of milk to the cooling room.

Our neighbor was lying on his back in the cow lot, a few feet from one milking parlor door. Rosebud, our herd bull, was standing over him threateningly and the man was paralyzed with fright, unable to move or even squeak.

As he ducked out of sight the last time, he had bumped into one of our cows, named Crump because of a crooked horn. He kicked at her and his shoe caught in the crook of that horn. Crump backed away, pulling him off his feet and into a pool of mud and juicy manure. Rosebud, who didn't like strangers either, trotted over to investigate.

Our neighbor was a pitiful sight as he left, reeking and dripping.

Next morning when Crump came in to be milked, Pop gave her an extra scoop of feed.

It was a pivotal day in my life, the one on which I left home for college. A hot September noontime and, dressed in my traveling clothes, I went to sit on the lid of the big cistern beside our barn. Maybelle, our Duroc sow, shuffled around the corner of the barn, greeted me with a "Howwwruff," and sniffed at my new shoes.

"Ronk," Maybelle said, meaning, "Make room for me."

I lifted my legs and she flopped in the cool weeds beside the cistern. I lowered my feet to her side and began moving them back and forth, gently scraping her bristly hide.

"Baawwrp," said Maybelle. It was a rumble of undiluted pleasure, the second happiest sound a sow can make.

I broke off a tall weed and used the butt of the stalk to scratch around Maybelle's uppermost ear.

"Ruuuunk-ruuuunk-ruunk-ruunk!" she crooned—a lullaby of pure delight. A sow will sometimes make the same statement when nursing its pigs on a clean warm bed of straw.

We sat for a time, scratching and communing. And our souls touched.

Everything in me, in the gold-and-green land around me, and in the wise and benign Maybelle flowed together and formed one ringing affirmation. This was where I belonged! This was my destiny!

"Don't believe I'll go to that dang college," I told Maybelle.

"Baawwrp," she replied, shifting her head so that I could scratch the other ear, "ruuuunk-ruuunk-ruunk-ruunk."

But as soon as I voiced the thought, it lost its magical lucidity and began to die. Like a sailfish pulled from the ocean it shed its glorious colors and in moments became dark and inert. Like many a fisherman, I realized too late what I had done. You cannot return a lifeless sailfish to the sea or an untimely dream to your soul.

I stood up. "Wheenk?" Maybelle grunted irritably. I walked away, to the pickup truck where my father waited, to a different destiny.

As we drove off, Maybelle sounded an alarm: "Woof, woof!" It's a danger signal, a warning to beware of strangers. In the hoglot, it is more than that. It is a rallying cry, a call to arms for mutual defense. "Stay here," Maybelle was telling me. "To thine own self be true and I will stand with you, hock to hock and jowl to jowl against all comers."

I never saw Maybelle again. She was a hog ahead of her time.

9/The sporting life

Once or twice a month during the baseball season, the conductor of the evening train would deliver a bundle of posters to the depot agent. He would tack one up and then send a boy scooting up the street to distribute the others to the grocery store, the town hall where a traveling projectionist showed movies every other Saturday and to the gas station and repair shop my father operated.

"DIZZY DEAN," the posters would shout in what printers called stud-horse type. Beneath the name, in smaller letters, it would say that Dizzy would pitch the following Saturday or Sunday in Sportsman's Park against such and such a team.

In those days of Depression a round-trip coach ticket to St. Louis, meals and a grandstand seat would just about ruin a $10 bill. A man would work a day for a dollar and his dinner, and be glad to get it, so an expenditure in two figures took a lot of thought.

One of my earliest memories is of standing barefoot in the dust at the edge of the street, resting my forearms on the edge of the high board sidewalk that ran in front of the town hall and listening to seven or eight adults, my father among them, talk about Dizzy. A new Cardinals poster had just been tacked up. The Giants would be the opponent.

Suddenly, in an elaborately casual tone, my father said, "I just might take in that game." Several sucked in their breath sharply and somebody said, "Hey, boy!" admiringly. I squinched my toes in ecstasy. I can still feel that cool dust squirting between them. I felt like yelling, but since Pop was playing it cool, I did too.

Don't misunderstand. I never entertained the notion for a second that I was going with him. Lordy! You could buy a cow and a calf for $10. But the honor and glory of having a father who'd just up and go to a ball game when he took a notion was overwhelming.

Pop's trip became more of a community project than a private excursion. As almost always happened after somebody broke the ice, two or three other men stopped at the station to say they'd decided to go, too.

Pop and the other voyageurs discussed travel arrangements. Since there was only one train a day to St. Louis and since they all lived within sight of the depot, there were no great logistical problems. Still, they talked of the matter at length.

The wives got together and decided who would pack what food for lunch on the train. Fried chicken and deviled eggs for everybody, they decided.

The men collected St. Louis papers for a week or two back and tried to figure out who would pitch against Diz. It might be Carl Hubbell but most probably Freddie Fitzsimmons, they decided after checking box scores to learn the rotation. Fat Freddie was a good one, but he had a sore arm.

No matter, give Diz one run and he'd beat anybody. Get the run himself, if he had to. The year before he'd won 30 games, lost 7 and clinched the pennant with two shutouts in three days at Cincinnati. Brother Paul won the middle game and then both brothers won two games in the World Series against the Tigers.

Veterans of the trip stopped at the station to talk of the games they had seen. Diz going up against Hubbell or Lon Warneke of the Cubs or Van Lingle Mungo of Brooklyn or Waite Hoyt, who was at Pittsburgh.

They always went to see Diz. For two reasons, probably. He was pure baseball player and he was country. Country all the way, even in those big cities and fancy hotels and talking to governors and all. They understood him. A good

old boy who never turned his back on them.

He was tall, about 6-foot-2, and lean and limber as a buggy whip in those days. His motion was smooth and graceful, I've been told a hundred times, and the ball would blur out of that easy windup with unexpected velocity. He had a big curve and little curves and the slider before anybody had named it. Some sharp-eyed country people who ought to know told me that his pitches weren't always perfectly dry. But whose were in those days? Or now?

Diz could set up a hitter and strike him out with the pitch he wanted to throw. But mostly he liked to use his infield.

Hitters would pound 'em into the dirt and Frankie Frisch and Leo Durocher and Rip Collins and Pepper Martin would scoop 'em up. Once in a while Diz would make a mistake and Terry Moore would climb the centerfield fence and haul it down. If Diz did give up a home run, you could almost bet that the bases were empty, because he hardly ever walked a man. He hit quite a few, though. He was mean.

When he got a lead, he might have some fun. They told him a certain batter murdered the curve low and away. So Diz struck him out three times, then with a safe lead, he tried the curve. The guy hit it seven miles. "You was sure right," Diz told his apopletic manager, Frisch.

Diz won that game my father went to. Fat Freddie didn't

pitch; it was a kid named Slick Castleman. Dad never saw Dizzy again, but he talked about him the rest of his life.

I never met Diz or saw him pitch, but when I heard that he had died after a heart attack, I could only think that it had been a great pleasure knowing him.

Bullet, my high-school football coach, got a pep talk every fall from Timberline Mitchell (he was bald on top) to the effect that it wasn't whether you won or lost or even how you played the game, but that the mark of a good coach was keeping the football budget under $550 per annum. Bullet, God love him, believed every word.

Timberline, the school superintendent, always worked in the story of the Praying Colonels of Centre College who, in his version, showed up barefoot and wearing "bib overhalls and whomped the goofer dust" out of Harvard. He told the same story to the team captains when they called on him after an angry squad meeting to ask whether the school couldn't pop for a few new uniforms or at least enough helmets to go around. Timberline bought outer uniforms about ninth hand from Ash Flat, Ark., Teachers College. The pads were, I believe, cut down from Civil War cavalry saddles. After every season, the coach took them home and, with an awl and leather strips, patched them.

Some of the helmets were leather and soft as an old first baseman's mitt. Fred Dixon wore his backwards once in a while. When it slid down over his eyes, he'd casually brush it back with one hand. Very disconcerting to a stranger across the line. It looked like Fred's head was lolling on a broken neck. When Shug came into a game, either Piggy or I had to leave because only two helmets fit the three of us.

Bullet, of course, suffered from a terminal case of dumb. But

even he would have wised up eventually if his vision hadn't
been blurred by ambition. Timberline was at retirement age
and he always confided to Bullet that the board was looking
for a young administrator who knew the value of a dollar.
Everybody in town except Bullet knew that the school board
was just waiting for Joe Bixby, son of the board chairman, to
get his master's degree from Cape Girardeau State.

Bullet did his best. He bought two new game balls a year
and kept them under lock and key. When opponents
warmed up, he roamed the sidelines kicking loose balls back
into the shadows in hopes that they would be overlooked.
Got two from Cabool one game. It cost $5 and five cents a
mile to hire a bus, so Bullet organized student car pools—
fun for the kids but occasionally it left him a few players shy
at game time.

At least twice a season, Bullet had to hire a bus. The trips to
Mountain Grove and Springfield (and inevitable defeat)
were too long to tempt student drivers. Bullet's misery
would be intensified because he had to provide a meal, too.
Once, Mrs. Bullet got hold of some huge cans of rubbery
pork scraps pressed together and given a cute name. She
made sandwiches and the manager of the Dr. Pepper bot-
tling plant contributed two cases of pop, but no ice. Arrgh!

The drive to Springfield on a narrow, dangerous Ozarks
highway took at least four hours, longer if we couldn't keep
Bullet's mind off the game. Bullet spent more time on his
budget than coaching, but on game day, remorse and excitement caught up with him. Especially with his kidneys. He'd
stop the bus every 15 minutes and wander into the woods,
then come back and work himself up again, telling us that
when the going got tough the tough got going and that
Springfield's Blue Devils pulled their pants on one leg at a
time.

The only way we could keep him quiet was for the team
swingers to move up front and tell him dirty jokes. At the
punch line, Bullet would wheeze, "Hee, hee, hee, you
scamp," then glance guiltily over his shoulder. On arrival he
vanished into the nearest john, emerging only to swipe
warm-up balls and for the kickoff.

One year we led Springfield 12-7 with less than two minutes to play when Piggy was knocked unconscious. They carried him off on a stretcher and sent him to a hospital. With his helmet on.

Bullet told Shug to get in there at defensive halfback, but the officials wouldn't let him on the field without a helmet. Bullet thought about pulling me from middle linebacker, but I already had my uniform muddied up, as he explained later, and using a fresh linebacker would have run up the laundry bill. He sent in a muddy sophomore with a helmet instead of Shug. Springfield started throwing and completed the third pass just over that sophomore's head. The guy scored.

Old Shug would have caught him.

Bullet operated on what he liked to call a "sowbelly and hardtack" budget of $550 per year. Some of his players brought their own footballs to practice. It was either that or run laps while the first string used the school ball.

Not that our school didn't own several footballs, but Bullet couldn't keep track of more than one at a time. On game nights when he had to break out three balls for warm-up, Bullet suited up three freshmen to watch them. Lose a ball and your athletic career ended forthwith.

One summer, though, Bullet decided to hang the expense and hold a summer football camp. Our archrival, Mountain Grove, had a camp every year and Bullet claimed that gave them the edge. Mountain Grove had beaten us in something like 48 consecutive games.

"I got the hosses and it's time to put this town on the football map," Bullet told our local sports editor. Astonished but delighted, the sportswriter trumpeted the news to equally astounded alumni. Bullet's best season previously was four victories, one by forfeit.

About 35 apprehensive kids gathered on the town square. We'd never been to camp, but we knew Bullet. The sports editor posed us for pictures and we climbed onto two trucks, sitting on the rolled-up tarps, blankets and extra clothing we'd brought. There was a stack of picks, shovels, mattocks, brush hooks and crosscut saws on each truck.

When we saw those tools, Billy Gates jumped off the truck, ran into the courthouse and enlisted in the navy. He had a fine time the next four years, about as long as it took the rest of us to recover from Bullet's camp.

The campsite was an abandoned summer home owned by one member of our school board. It was on a creek about 25 miles from town, the last three down a rutted, one-lane trail that the woods had almost reclaimed. The creek itself was a sluggish trickle, flowing over sharp rocks and gravel to gather in a fetid pool about three feet deep just in front of the house. Two water moccasins, poisonous snakes also known as cottonmouths, called that pool home.

The house was padlocked fore and aft and the windows were nailed shut. Bullet set up a cot for himself in a little lean-to behind the house. There was an old wood stove there for cooking. There were no restroom facilities. No outhouse. Nothing. Just miles and miles of woods.

The first afternoon was spent clearing a sleeping area. The yard and creek bottom had grown up in briars, brush and sprouts, which is what we call saplings. Wild grape vines covered everything. We'd cut a dozen saplings and a batch of blackberry briars and discover they were held together by an enormous network of vines.

By the time we had hacked out places to spread our tarps and blankets, Bullet and the team captains had cooked supper. Beans and franks, boiled for hours into a gummy, rust-colored sludge. It was the best meal we had all week.

There were no lights, no lamps or lanterns. "Can't think of
everything," Bullet explained. So we built fires. We needed
them. The smoke helped keep the mosquitoes at bay.
"Throw on some wet leaves," Bullet advised. "Makes a good
smudge."

Next morning Bullet split us into two units. "Seniors and
freshmen work on the road," he said. "I wanna see them
chogholes filled in. Wanna ride out of here on a super-
highway. Juniors and sophomores get this meadow cleaned
up. Pile that brush up neat, now." Then Bullet returned to
his cot to work on his playbook.

The woods beside the road were full of ticks. The brush was
full of chiggers. Next day we switched assignments and
everybody got some ticks to keep his chiggers company or
vice versa.

Late on the third day, Bullet brought out a football and held
a passing drill. His quarterback had some sort of ear infec-
tion from swimming in the creek. Felt like water sloshing
around in his head, he said. If he tried to straighten up
quickly, he lost balance and fell on his side. His passing was
a bit erratic.

The first receiver to actually get his hands on a pass
screamed and dropped the ball. After using a brush hook for
two days he had blisters on top of blisters.

It was a short workout. What with dodging stumps and stubs
of briars, stubbing our toes on rocks and getting tangled in
vines, it was hard to achieve a slow trot.

Three guys went over the hill that night. Walked to the
highway and hitch-hiked home. The rest of us were in a
stupor, too weak to care.

Next morning the sidemeat Bullet had been frying for
breakfast was a little moldy. He scraped it clean and cooked
it anyway. Within an hour we were all throwing up.

"Work it off," Bullet kept saying. "Keep moving. A little

pukin' cleans out the system." But by noon he gave up,
loaded us on the trucks and took us home.

Bullet tried to set us an example. Every fall when football
practice started, he would stop buying beer at the liquor
store and have Eli, the town bootlegger, deliver it to his
house until the season ended.

Eli obliged, but grudgingly. He discouraged one-shot orders
and seasonal trade, preferring to stick with his regulars, who
included the racy country club set, two bank officers, each of
whom did not want the other to know that he drank, and a
few dazed middle management types transferred to our
town when a shoe company built a factory to tap a pool of
cheap Ozark labor.

Eli had no problem of supply. He was part owner of the
legal liquor store. Nor did he fear the local law. He'd been
on the force himself until his sideline grew into a full-time
occupation. His former colleagues sometimes helped with
deliveries when business piled up at New Year's or on the
weekend quail season opened.

Eli's problem was parking. Most everybody in town knew
his car and he'd better not leave it outside their house. Mrs.
Eli got angry calls from her best friend when Eli's battery
went dead and his car sat out front overnight. Also, Bullet
and most of Eli's regular customers made him take away
their empties. They didn't want the garbage haulers to find
them. The feeling around town was that when a drinker
started leaving empties for the trashmen, he had lost all
pride and was past redemption. Merchants might start press-
ing a tippler like that to settle his accounts.

Eli had the instincts of a merchant prince. He provided a
unique service, gave satisfaction, was discreet (was it his

fault that everyone in town knew his car?) and therefore was not ashamed to charge a handsome price for his wares. Usually Eli was paid on delivery, but he would extend credit. Collecting was no problem. The thought of Eli dropping in at the office was enough to make a customer's blood run cold.

Eli made most deliveries at night, parking a block or so from the client's home and cutting across lots or down alleys. He carried a pocketful of weiners to placate dogs.

Every so often somebody would report him as a prowler and once he had a really hairy experience. That was the night police and sheriff's deputies broke up their pitch game to catch a sex fiend.

Somebody had spotted the sex fiend peeping into windows nearly every night for a week. This time a caller had seen the fiend slipping down an alley and believed he was still in there. In a matter of minutes officers had the alley sealed off. The chief sent Jaydee, a short wiry patrolman, in from one end and Hake, a fat, hulking sergeant, from the other.

After a short wait, there were grunts, screams and the sound of running feet. Jaydee and Hake emerged simultaneously from opposite ends of the alley. "Big slob," Jaydee panted. "Got away from me, I think he's got a knife." Meanwhile, Hake was reporting, "Skinny little devil. I'd a had him if I hadn't tripped."

About then Eli sauntered from the alley to inquire amiably what the fuss was about. He had been standing by a fence, responding to a call of nature, when two men tiptoed into view. They spotted each other at the same instant and froze for a second. "Then both of 'em screeched and lit out," Eli said.

Jaydee wanted to run Eli in on sex charges. Hake wanted to search his car for contraband. The chief, disgusted, sent Eli home and went back to his pitch game. They never did catch that sex fiend.

My friend Gene was a fighter of some competence and for several years after World War II was the favorite sparring partner of featherweight champion Willie Pep. Gene also was one of the few non-Oriental chick sexers to be found in the Ozark region, a fact that has always fascinated me and which has no bearing on any other portion of this tale.

Late one evening I was sipping a cherry phosphate in the Cinderella Confectionery and listening to Tex Ritter's recording of "Smoke, Smoke, Smoke" when Gene slid onto the stool beside me and said, "Gimme a lift down to the Frisco siding. I want to check an investment."

A man with high-octane sporting blood had two major outlets in my hometown: Occasional cockfights in a barn near Viola, Ark., or Saturday night crap games in an empty boxcar on a Frisco sidetrack down by the Farmers Exchange. On that night perhaps 15 men were rolling 'em by the light of a kerosene lantern. Most of the group were sawmill hands from Birchtree, in for a monthly fling.

Gene really was watching an investment. Clinton, a handsome, dark-sideburned, bucolic bon vivant in pleated gabardine slacks and two-toned wingtip oxfords, had borrowed $10 from Gene and had the dice. Beside him was his inseparable companion, a rugged chap called Romey, who for a quarter, would let you break a two-by-four over his skull, hitting him with the wide surface.

Luck smiled on Clinton. Dollar bills and the odd five-spot piled up in the lamplight as he made point after point. A sawmill hand watching a month's pay flutter toward a slick stranger is a volatile quantity and Clinton knew it well.

"I ought to be getting home," he remarked uneasily.

"If I had your money, I'd go too," growled one of the losers.

The lantern went out!

Grunts, the thud of blows and scuffling sounds filled the next several seconds. Then one of the sawmill hands switched on a flashlight. He and his companions hadn't moved. Clinton was astraddle his pal Romey, choking him with one hand and pounding him with a fistful of bills.

Gene introduced me to Clinton, collected his $10 and, as we drove back to the town square, explained that Clinton, a middleweight who had retired seven or eight years earlier, was making a comeback under Gene's management. Further, Willie Pep had summoned Gene and I had been chosen to oversee Clinton's training during Gene's absence and to deliver him to a nearby town for his first comeback appearance two Saturdays hence.

That was Saturday night. About 3 a.m. Monday Clinton pounded on my door. He was broke, drunk and homeless. His winnings hadn't lasted long enough to get him even with his landlady. For the next two weeks, Clinton slept in my bed. He ate at my expense, having already cashed in the meal tickets Gene had provided. He found a spare set of keys and borrowed my car, abandoning it 25 miles from home, out of gas. He couldn't buy gas because he'd already spent the money he got for hocking my radio and topcoat.

I delivered Clinton each morning to the local armory, where he trained, and saw him set off on his five miles of roadwork along a narrow country road. Curiously, Clinton did not object to this drudgery. Early the second week I learned why.

For some reason, I had returned to the armory and, not finding Clinton, was leaving when some heavy object smashed against the big side door used for National Guard trucks. It was Clinton. On a bicycle. So drunk he couldn't see through a stepladder. About a quarter of a mile from the armory, a path led through the woods from that country road to a state highway and the grounds of a roadhouse whose buxom, middle-aged owner much admired Clinton. It had been his custom to jog along the path, relax for an hour or so, then trot back, working up a light sweat. That morning he indulged too heavily, lingered too long and borrowed a bicycle to return. His reflexes and the bicycle's brakes both failed near the armory door.

Clinton's fight was in a town about 60 miles away. When he and Romey and I set off, Clinton confided that he was a little nervous. He had a large sack of cookies, which he munched steadily. Those and occasional nips from a pint of whiskey improved his spirits. (If you had been in my place, would you have tried to stop him? I was hoping he'd be killed.)

We stopped on the town's main street to get directions to the fairgrounds where the fight would be held. I stopped a man leaving a cafe—a short, pudgy, middle-aged man with a fringe of reddish-gray hair. The man had just told me how to get there when Clinton lurched up beside me, put a hand on my shoulder, leaned over and threw up all over the fellow's trousers and shoes.

Four hours later Clinton and I stood near the rear of the arena while the referee for the professional card was introduced—a short, pudgy, middle-aged man with a fringe of reddish-gray hair.

The next evening I was sipping a cherry phosphate in the Cinderella and listening to a song about a mining camp gal who wore red silk stockings and green perfume when Gene slid onto the next stool.

"Everything go all right?" he asked.

The story they told on Slop was that he showed up a few years after World War I and bought a dab of land just outside the county seat. He raised hogs and ran a garbage route with a mule-drawn wagon loaded with barrels. He'd start out with a few gallons of water in each barrel and dump his gatherings from cafes, boarding houses and grocery stores right in. The jouncing would agitate the gruel nicely, so that when he got home in mid-afternoon it was ready to pour.

The water also helped cut the smell, Slop said. Trouble was, Slop wasn't under water. He'd wear one pair of bib overalls until it was rotten. Some summer days it was hard to choose whether you'd rather have Slop come around or just keep your garbage.

When banks started to fail in the Depression, the story continues, Slop shed his overalls, called on the local banker and revealed himself as a graduate with honors from Harvard Business. (I got this story from Grandma Bandy and Charlie Jones, both.) Slop went to work for the bank and pulled 'er through. Then he put his overalls back on and hitched up his mules. From then until his death, Slop never referred to those years of working in the bank. The only change in his life-style in later years was putting rubber tires on his wagon.

Rumor had it that Slop's house was full of books, but his only visible recreation was baseball. He was an encyclopedia of major league names, batting averages, pitching records, World Series, rules. His mules knew the route and Slop would wrap the reins around a wagon stake and commit the Sporting News to memory each week.

Baseball is a country game. In the Ozarks in Slop's time it was a Sunday game for teams of grown men. Challenge matches in crossroads pastures with chicken-wire backstops and red clay pitching mounds. Cars would be parked along the baselines, but back a ways. If Beano Martin, a powerful pull hitter was playing, nobody parked near third base. Small boys would be stationed in the fringes of scrub oak and sassafrass around the outfield to hunt for balls.

These games were bitterly contested. A man who had cut sprouts or chopped cotton or put up hay all week had a lot of aggression to unload. Moreover, teams usually were made up from clans or from neighbors and there would be old

grudges to work off against that day's opponent. When Peace Valley and Hammond's Mill played, you could generally count on a fight. If the game didn't provide cause, one of the big-eyed girls switching around in a summer dress or sitting on a car hood sipping Dr. Pepper would.

Slop attended a country ball game every Sunday. He knew all the players, just as he had known their fathers and uncles. He could look at a strange youth and correctly identify him as a Southfork Collins or a Dripping Springs Jolliff by the way he broke off a curve ("inshoots" and "drops" and "outcurves" were mentioned) or swung a bat.

Slop would be there before anyone else. Wagon in a good spot, mules tied in the shade, his working overalls exchanged for a fresh pair. He'd already have earned his keep with his scoop shovel.

Managers of country teams carry scoops in their pickups. Cows are pastured on the fields during the week and the infield must be tidied up, thistles gouged out and the pitching mound repaired. Slop would do all of these things before anyone else arrived. Then he would lean back against his wagon and wait. His vast knowledge was available on request, but he never pushed himself into a conversation.

A hat would usually be passed during the seventh inning

and the players on the winning team would split the money. All except the pitchers. Most of them were mercenaries. Win or lose, they were paid a set fee by the farmer or storekeeper or whoever sponsored the team. Slop often was called in to set the fee when manager and pitchers could not agree.

A top pitcher got top dollar, although the amount would vary according to the team. The Moody store owner was known to be rich and top dollar at Moody might be $25, while the scale elsewhere for the same pitcher might be $15. The important thing was that he got top money both places. When Slop suggested a lower rate, that pitcher knew that his career was waning. Many simply quit. Some swallowed their pride and took the cut.

But nobody ever argued with Slop.

10/Sex and the country boy

Up to somewhere near age 11 my romantic life consisted of daydreams in which I rescued favorite teachers from assorted knaves. Generally I would arrive in the nick of time astride a magnificent black horse.

Then I met Alice. I had been deposited at my grandparents' farm for a visit. Alice and her folks, shirt-tail kin to my grandmother, were staying there, too. Alice was two or three years older than I and beautiful. She would ruffle my hair or blow in my ear and I would turn to butter. I knew nothing about romance, but I knew what I liked.

To get right down to it, one day I was fooling around in the barn with my Buck Rogers pistol, which whirred and spat sparks. Alice came tripping from the house and I decided to show her how I felt about her.

I hid near the barn door and let Alice pass me. Leaping from cover with a screech, I blazed away with my Buck Rogers pistol.

I just thought I had screeched. Alice showed me how it should be done. Then she darted from the barn, shrieking and sobbing. I followed, mouth open.

Magically, people appeared from everywhere, the house, sheds, the grape arbor. There were my grandmother, Aunt Lena, Alice's mother, Uncle Olen and two or three cousins, neighbor Jim Walker and his wife, visiting from down by the river.

"Nasty, nasty, nasty!" Alice screamed, pointing at me. "He was nasty!"

Nasty! In a barn! Everybody knew what that entailed, everyone but me, and I would be enlightened shortly.

Alice's father came from nowhere, blotting out the sky. He shook me until my teeth hurt. One of my shoes fell off and the Buck Rogers pistol flew somewhere. I never found it.

By then everyone was in the house, where I was dragged. When she saw me, Alice started squawking "nasty, nasty" again. Olen, who has always had a passion for detail, asked just what happened, but Alice sobbed and hid her face in her mother's bosom. The others apparently preferred to fill in the blank spaces themselves.

By now, of course, Alice was enjoying the attention. And, though I hate to give her credit, I imagine that things rapidly got to the point where she was afraid to back up and tell it straight. I was stunned, witless, full of horrible guilt. I would have confessed to mass murder, arson or the Lindbergh kidnaping.

My grandfather, Poppy, was in his usual place, a hickory rocker by the stove. Eventually he would sort things out and decide my fate, but for now he told me to go shell corn for the chickens.

I shelled until I was called to supper. I sat on the children's bench Alice previously had shared with me. Now she was huddled near her mother.

"Hush now, just hush and eat," Poppy said when Alice's mother began to scold me, but she wouldn't be squelched. "Somebody's got to tell this brat," she said, "that if he keeps up his dirty ways, he'll get a baby."

Holy smoke! What had I done? I nearly died right there, but

managed to run into the bedroom I shared with Poppy. My grandmother threw her apron over her head and tottered into the kitchen. I could hear her crying as I sat on the bed.

Now, I was dumb but country. I knew about birds, bees, cows and hogs. But I had never equated ladyfolk with livestock. It might be possible to get one of them in the family way by scaring her silly. I knew that girls' mothers were always hollering out the door at them to be careful. Maybe that was why.

When Poppy came to bed, he smoked a final pipe while listening to gospel music on the radio. Normally he would turn off the radio and go to sleep immediately, but this night he softly sang a couple of lines of "Cotton Eyed Joe," his signal that he was available for conversation.

I asked him if you could make a baby by scaring a girl in a barn.

"I've heard of cases," Poppy said. "Depends on how you go at it."

I told him I hid behind the feed bin and came out shooting and hollering.

"Well then," said Poppy, "that hain't the way it's done. Put the whole thing out of your mind."

Greatly comforted, I went to sleep.

The first day after my buddy Jack got a job as lifeguard at our town's swimming pool, he discovered a loose knot in the wall of the girls' dressing room. After Jack worked on it a little bit with his pocketknife, the knot could be lifted out to provide a peephole, then replaced. He spread the word.

The knothole got a big play. Pool receipts soared, even with Jack dipping into them for Dr. Pepper and Eskimo Pie money. If a fellow didn't have time to swim, he'd drop by for a viewing—sauntering around the corner from the shallow end while a confederate kept watch.

Freddie, our school's leading feeb, spent so much time at the pool that he lost his pimples and acquired a nice tan. For several years, Freddie had spent his waking hours in the pool hall, emerging only when an Esther Williams movie played our town. Consequently, his complexion was a light green set off by dozens of red splotches.

Some zesty tales were told that summer at the Cinderella Confectionery and repeated and embellished over the snooker tables at the Business Men's Club. Jack and I figured that several young ladies received proposals of marriage strictly on word-of-mouth advertising. And a good many friendships were struck up by youths who had previously hesitated to buy a pig in a poke.

One day the following winter, Jack remembered that he had never turned in his key to the poolhouse. We drove to the deserted park, went in and looked around.

The knothole, we discovered, pierced the back wall of a cupboard full of mops, brooms, cleaning rags, wornout swimsuits and the like. The cupboard had no top or door, so it was dimly lit and the shadows admittedly could have been confusing.

But almost all of those glimpses of girlflesh, those steamy tales we told and listened to, were products of our overheated imaginations. We had manufactured them from old mops and rags, and from dimly heard squeals and splashes and giggles.

Gooorrrd! How embarrassing!

Almost 20 years later Miller and I met by chance. Neither of us, each admitted, had ever told a soul the truth about that knothole.

Knowing the truth, we still halfway believed that we had
seen something. How could it have happened? Freddie, a
real goof who had been busted out of several private
schools, probably had as much to do with the mass hypnosis
as anyone, we decided. When Freddie was well launched
into one of his descriptions, we'd have to push him back
from the pool table so he wouldn't drool on the felt.

Nobody wanted to be out-lewded by a dip like Freddie.

Technique had something to do with it, too. The practice
was to peer through the knothole until you thought you saw
something in the murky interior then dash around the
corner to see who emerged from the dressing room. Clearly,
fantasy and fact had blended.

Jack contemplated with some satisfaction and awe the forces
he had set into motion. Sitting there in a car on courthouse
square, we could see children of couples who had gotten
together because of his keen eye and dexterity with a
pocketknife. Did a future senator, a president, an astronaut
owe existence to Jack?

What would happen, we wondered, if we told?

Ramona Sue was the best looking girl in school with the
possible exception of Mary Elizabeth, who dated only starting quarterbacks or the occasional halfback who had a good
game. (Just to clear up the point, we lived far enough south
so that all the girls and most of the boys used two front
names. Our mothers had practically memorized the novels
of Helen Hunt Jackson, so names like Ramona were common, too.)

Ramona Sue played the drum in the school marching band
and therefore was on display at all home games and some of

those in nearby towns. I pinned my hopes on those road games.

It was the amiable and economical custom of our football coach, Bullet, to permit team members of good character to drive their own cars to nearby games. Not infrequently enough players did this—in carload lots of four or five—to enable Bullet to dispense with hiring a bus.

I had never been regarded by Bullet as being of good character. It started with his nickname. When he was hired, word spread around town that he had been called "Bullet" at Cape Girardeau State because of the velocity and accuracy of his passes. Bullet did not deny the rumor. But I happened to learn, and let him know I knew, that his teammates really had called him "Shotgun," because after 10 yards his throws were apt to veer anywhichway.

My plan had the simplicity which marked Bonaparte's more successful campaigns. I had become owner of a '39 DeSoto which, since my father was a master mechanic, ran well enough. I would establish myself with Bullet as a lad of strong moral fiber, obtain his permission to drive to a road game, then ask Ramona Sue to ride back with me. Riding BACK was the key. Under school rules she would have to take the band bus to the game. It wasn't unheard of for one of the band girls to drive home with her swain, but it still was daring enough to appeal to a girl of spirit.

It took several weeks to bring Bullet around. I started calling him "Sir," asked a lot of questions in my most sincere manner and yelled "Darn right!" every time he made a point. Still the Willow Springs and Cabool trips went by and there was left only the game at Mountain View when Bullet caved in.

Ramona Sue capitulated when I cunningly asked whether her bandmates would be shocked. Wow! I bought a package of Sen-Sen and set aside my best pair of argyle socks.

After the game, I was a blur of motion from field to locker room to my car where Ramona Sue waited.

With her drum.

For those of you who are not old-car buffs, let me say that a bass drum will not fit into the trunk of a 1939 DeSoto coupe. The only place it will go is right in the middle of the seat, provided the driver and his passenger each scrunch painfully against a doorhandle. Conversation is possible, of course, but driver and passenger cannot see each other, much less touch.

The night was young and worse lay ahead. About a mile down the road the engine had warmed up and I switched on the heater. Slowly a nauseating, unbearable stench filled the car. I stopped and checked everything but couldn't find the source. It was a little better if we switched off the heater, but still after another mile or so, we had to roll down the windows. Our hands and feet grew numb.

We had 25 miles to cover and the first 15 passed in complete silence. Then I croaked inanely, "You there?"

"Oh God, am I ever!" Ramona Sue replied.

As we neared town I suggested that hot chocolate at the Cinderella Confectionery might thaw us out. "Why don't you get some after you take me home," she snapped.

The next day she told everyone in school that I apparently had been hauling hogs to market in my car. She began dating Jimmy Bob Wallace, who had unlimited use of his father's pickup. They later married.

Some time afterward, Jimmy Bob confessed that he had smeared limburger cheese all over the manifold and heater of my car.

———————————

Army surplus coveralls were "in" that final year of high school. We bought them stiff and green from the surplus store, coaxed our mothers to wash and rewash them, with a little bleach, and abused them dreadfully. The idea was to make them look like battle gear, the rips and stains taken for combat scars.

We would buy an Army web belt with a brass buckle and cinch it tightly at the waist. On most of us, the waist was the only place the coveralls touched. Garish argyle socks encased our ankles. I tell you, we were dangerous-looking studs.

The owner of the surplus store caught on swiftly. He would take the new coveralls he received, stencil serial numbers on them and wash them and scrub them with a wire brush until they were suitably frayed and faded. Then he would raise the price $2.

He couldn't keep up with the demand. No telling where these ol' coveralls been, we would tell each other. The Solomon Islands, Iwo Jima, into Germany with Patton.

"Slam books" were in vogue that year, too. A slam book was an autograph album, converted, or more accurately, perverted to another use. The owner of a slam book would write the names of various schoolmates in it, one to a page, and leave it in a convenient place, usually on an unoccupied table in study hall. Anyone could read a slam book and write in it.

The idea was to write a terse, unsigned comment on the person whose name headed the page. Entries tended to be scaldingly frank. Your innermost secrets, which you thought you had concealed from the world, were spread out there for all to read.

The only thing more embarrassing than reading about yourself in a slam book was being left out of it. That meant you were beneath notice. Occasionally a suffering outcast would find a blank page and write his name on it. Usually the owner of the book, retrieving it after study hall, would note under the name that she (only girls kept slam books though everyone read them) hadn't listed this person. The young are openly cruel. Later on we become sly.

Slam books catalogued the inception, progress and break-up of dozens of school romances. Indeed, they were responsible for many of them. Writing anonymously, you could craftily indicate interest in some princess in penny loafers and ankle bracelet. That person's friends would swiftly inform her that somebody had noticed that somebody else in American History couldn't keep his eyes on the blackboard. Or she would read it herself. Sometimes the spark fell on dry tinder.

Romance was always on our minds. My own heart was broken three times before basketball season that year. I began these affairs well, but they faded swiftly. I never understood why. Consequently, I spent most of my time in the early throes of passion or in a fog of bewilderment.

A slam book chronicled one of my romantic ventures in a single entry. From tender beginning to frosty parting, it lasted only a few hours. Swift, even for me.

I escorted a lovely young lady to the movies. As we waited for the feature to begin, she told me that an aunt in Memphis had sent her a bottle of cologne. She leaned close so that I could sniff her adorable ear.

My senses reeled, but I realized that I should try to keep the intimate mood alive. I groped for a response and somewhere in the murky recesses of my overheated brain a memory stirred.

Did you know, I asked her, that Cleopatra used crocodile dung as a cosmetic?

The question aroused considerable interest in the seats around us but none at all in the young lady.

Actually, I said, trying to retrieve the situation, Cleopatra used it as a contraceptive.

A couple of days later the whole incident was recorded in a slam book. In red ink.

Two things never fail to make me blush: Recalling the words of my high school song and reading my high school yearbook. Improbable as it may seem, our school teams were named the Zizzers. The song begins "Zizzers, Zzziiiizzzzerrrs, faithful to . . ." and gets worse. I have never attended a class reunion.

The yearbook is one long leatherbound embarrassment. I can't get through two pages without wishing that I knew then what I know now. And then I have to ask, what do I know now?

Well, I know enough not to let a fickle, brown-eyed girl named Ellasue wangle my class ring away from me in the Cinderella Confectionery and wear it like a trophy for a week and then drop it in my lap and go off with Leon Tate— a mighty fine pulling guard, I have to give him that, though a little weak on pass blocking—while my heart cracks into three pieces.

That much I know. And a fat lot of good it did me, except in

the matter of that chunk of post oak on our woodpile.

That hunk of wood was sawed from the crotch of a post oak tree. It was twisted, knotted and burled. It was too big to burn whole in our heating stove, too tough and bent-grained to split and too crooked to use as a chopping block. It just lay there on the pile, a perpetual aggravation. It won't even fit comfortably in this memory, though it belongs here. Leave it there on the pile until it's needed and move on to the matter of class rings.

Class rings were purchased during the junior year. Delivery day was a big event and for a few weeks thereafter not a whole lot of serious scholastic work got done around school. One by one, the boys' rings would be bestowed on girls, wrapped with tape to fit a smaller finger or dangling on a chain around the young lady's throat.

It was a solemn affair, this gift of a ring. A class ring was Forever, often clear through basketball season.

Ellasue turned those brown eyes on me one afternoon at the Cinderella and I nearly drowned in them. I went home in a happy daze, without my ring.

We spent a lot of time together in the week that followed, meeting between classes and after football practice. If Ellasue seemed, well, less committed than I, I laid it to her enchanting ladylike ways.

Came Friday, the day of the annual spring football game, which matched graduating seniors and freshmen against juniors and sophomores. It was played right after school and always drew a large crowd, since it gave local fans a chance to see next year's varsity in a game that it was certain to win. It would also be the occasion of my first real date with Ellasue.

Traditionally, players and their girls met at the Cinderella after the game. There would be Cokes and sandwiches, a good deal of cruising around town in packed cars, a movie. The game would be replayed endlessly, the defeated seniors would be gracious. An altogether happy evening.

I took my time showering and dressing. Leon stopped beside me, ruffled my hair and told me that I had played well. I had, but Leon was more complimentary than necessary. Vaguely, I wondered why.

When I reached the Cinderella, Ellasue was there. With Leon. Unmistakably with Leon. She was not wearing my ring! Forever had lasted seven days.

I sat in a back booth, ordered a large chocolate Coke and drank it without tasting it. Ellasue came back after a while, patted my shoulder and told me that she would always remember me. She dropped my class ring in my lap.

I drove around for a while with some guys, watched part of the movie—Greer Garson and Clark Gable—and eventually headed home, eight miles through the hills. I stopped at Elk Pond and sat beside it until it got light enough to make out the lily pads. Pretty near milking time. I went on home.

That blasted old hunk of oak caught my eye when I got out of the car. I grabbed the axe and buried it in the chunk. I raised it over my head and hammered it against the chopping log—five, ten, fifty times. It cracked and split in half. I laid the halves on the chopping log and split them into kindling and that into splinters.

When I finished, I looked up and saw my father sitting on the top step of the back porch. I didn't know what to say. I stood there, my best clothes soaked with sweat, and threw out my arms in a gesture of helplessness.

Pop nodded sympathetically and then grinned.

"I wish," he said, "that I could point you at something necessary."